Living in the Fast Lane

Goodwood – memories and back...

by Michael Grace de'Udy

AuthorHouse™
1663 Liberty Drive
Bloomington, IN 47403
www.authorhouse.com
Phone: 1-800-839-8640

© 2013 Michael Grace de'Udy. All Rights Reserved.

No part of this book may be reproduced, stored in a retrieval system,
or transmitted by any means without the written permission of the author.

Published by AuthorHouse 04/10/2013

ISBN: 978-1-4817-8469-6 (sc)
978-1-4817-8470-2 (e)

The book author retains sole copyright to
his contributions to this book.
Photos from the author's private collection.

Other titles by the same author
My side of the Story

This book is printed on acid-free paper.

Because of the dynamic nature of the Internet, any web addresses or links contained in this book may have changed since publication and may no longer be valid. The views expressed in this work are solely those of the author and do not necessarily reflect the views of the publisher, and the publisher hereby disclaims any responsibility for them.

David Piper, myself and Corinne Goosens. My one and only race in a Ferrari, 1965

I would like to dedicate this book to Arabella and Daniel,
for putting up with me and my occasional outbursts
and in memory of Betty, Martin and Wally Ward,
without them none of this would have been possible.

Photographs from the author's private collection
Dictated in the Year 2000 – published with Authorhouse 2013

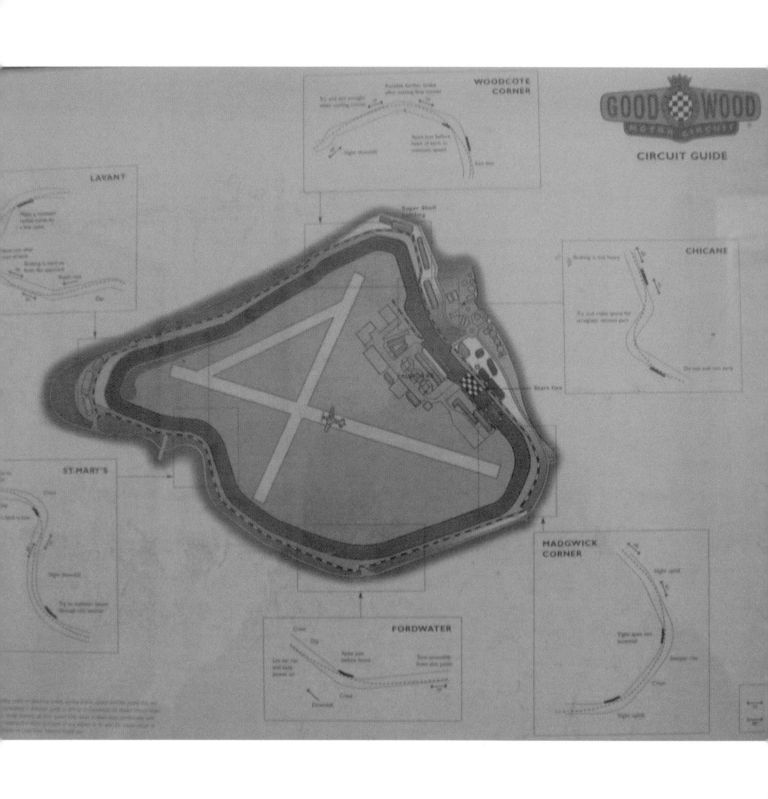

GOODWOOD - memories and back...

So this was the beginning of motor racing for me, and the end. Goodwood. The date is the 10th August in the year 2000 and I'm approaching the old bank I used to stand on many, many years ago to watch the likes of Archie Scott Brown, Stirling Moss, Ivor Bueb, Mike Hawthorn and Peter Collins, all legends in their own time and, for me in some ways, the greatest of all at Goodwood, Roy Salvadori.

He drove everything. He had a particular attitude in his driving and he enjoyed every moment of it. He was a bit hairy but he had the ability to beat everyone. He never became a World Champion, I don't think he wanted to. He could have. He was about thirty as I recall in the early days. Aston Martin, the very name raises one's motor racing hackles. That noise it made. I used to watch these things haring through here at all kinds of speeds.

Stirling Moss might have been quicker in the Jaguar from time to time and the Ferrari, but really this was Aston's place. Salvadori did all the testing here. It was just magnificent to watch, in particular the DBR1-300 and the Zagatos. Finally they ran out of ideas and kept using the same stuff over and over again; heavy, underpowered DB 485's I think they called them.

Still Salvadori was a soldier. He rolled these things on two wheels, he slid them through the Chicane and sometimes went off. They were totally outclassed by the Ferrari GTO at that stage, but he was the greatest to watch. Then Aston stopped racing. The tragedy was they decided to go into Formula 1 and as usual they were too slow. They took too long to develop the car but in the end they produced this magnificent looking, Salvadori driven, 2.5-litre front engine model, when all the other cars had been rear wheel drive, rear engined with a rear gearbox for two years; that was the configuration. Poor old Aston just wasn't up to it in any way, so Aston stopped.

Salvadori joined Cooper and now, standing here in the pits, I'm thinking this was never the track for me. It was a strange indulgence and total escape, when you have arrived at this track, this circuit the world is left behind. It's the most effective and the most successful means of escape I know, the rest of the world just does not even have access to this place. Lord March is rebuilding the grandstands, which used to be opposite the pits here 30 years ago and they have removed the old Chicane. At the grandstands of Woodcote there was a Super Shell billboard. I had one of my best shunts here in a Porsche 904, dicing with a lightweight E-type, which was quite a bit quicker but not through the corners - the right-hander.

This famous circuit was, I always maintain, designed by somebody who wished upon the competitor, destruction. Every bend here has a double apex, which sometimes cambers away from you, like Fordwater where Stirling Moss nearly died. Another legend in his own time.

I, myself, had my coup-de-gras just before the Chicane with the 904 when I dived inside this E-type driven by Peter Lumsden. It was a special lightweight. I did it all wrong. Got through the first bend all right, but the second, a nasty right-hander undid us so I had to spin the little 904 right around backwards into the bank. Shortened it by several inches in fact! Emerged, myself, totally unscathed, but rather sadly wrote the car off because it hit the bank with such a whack that its little ladder chassis was completely thrown out of alignment. The next day we had been due to send it off to Monza for the 1000K's. I was going to drive with Umberto Maglioli, but I threw it all away, in total and utter disgrace with Don Moore and his merry mechanics [ex Lister Jaguar]. I had many shunts in my 10 years of motor racing. Bad judgement. Never quite knew the right place to make that big shove. I usually did it in the wrong place at the wrong time and emerged with a total wreck and sometimes in hospital.

This was certainly my little taste of Goodwood. I never liked the damn place and of course I could never get over that Easter Monday when Stirling Moss, a person of absolutely incredible ability, talent and bravado, very nearly met his end here. He was such a good driver that there was really nobody else around for him to compete against. He competed therefore against himself and his lap times. He was called Mr. Motor Racing by the competition. The public would just come and enthral at watching these incredible feats but, on this one particular day and as usual driving for Rob Walker, he made several pit stops and fell fairly well behind.

Always, the highlight of the show was watching Moss catch up and overtake all the others. This time he didn't. He was in the process of roaring round Fordwater and then... off. Probably the throttle jammed open but Graham [B.R.M.] Hill saw it all happen. He went left round Graham Hill, then through a very gentle right-hander with the gradient slightly sliding away from you and off he went into this earth bank. He hit it head-on at 120 mph. Most people would have been killed by the sheer G's involved, but it took a friend of mine, George Arnold who worked the Blue Star Garage's towing truck, half an hour to cut him out of this wreckage. I had worked with the Blue Star Garage's manager, Charles Page, for a year and the big bonus of driving the old Chevy tow truck was that you got free tickets to pit and tow these wreckages off, so you had the absolute front row stand on the track.

George knew all this, so I would go on these adventures with him. On this particular day I'd left work early as I was sort of on my way up, climbing the ladder from the very very bottom, at the Jim Russell Racing Drivers School at Snetterton.

I walked around and saw the pitiful sight of this Lotus 19, shaped like an 'L'. Moss's legs and feet were in the 'L' part, which was now facing vertically in the air, whereas the long part of the 'L' containing the engine, the rear wheels and the driving compartment was absolutely parallel to the ground, about an inch above it. Anyway, he did survive this accident but of course was never the same person again. He tried to get back into racing, but found quite a lot of his equipment didn't function properly to his satisfaction, nor his eyesight.

He was a very interesting man. I had a chat with him at Kyalami, where he said that whenever he took his eyes off a particular object and moved them to another, that whole intervening period would be a blur. Eyesight is clearly No. 1 here, the connection between life and death and also peripheral vision. You can't really afford to move your eyes and not have perfect edges, or camber, in sight as well. So that was the end for him, "tunnel vision".

We watched them come and go. The most memorable day probably for me was watching Archie Scott Brown in the Lister Jag actually beat Stirling Moss in the DBR 1-300. Raymond Baxter was commentating. Again I think this happened near Fordwater, somewhere where you absolutely do not overtake because all these bends are designed intentionally to tighten for a 2.4-mile track, almost worse than the Nürburgring. There are so many people who have been killed here, including the late, great Bruce McLaren, because even the little straight here has a kink in it resulting in the fact that you can't see through it. So, as you come bombing down you aim for the kink, which at this point is your maximum depth of vision, and you hope there is nothing in the way as you go through it, flat out, without thinking of lifting off the gas pedal.

His rear engine cover on the McLaren, reckoned to be doing pretty near 200mph being the very latest Can-Am, came unclasped because the rubber clips hadn't been properly fastened in the pit stop. It was a private testing session, up came the fibreglass, off went the car and McLaren went somersaulting off into the field. He never knew what hit him. A totally unnecessary sort of accident and one which would not have taken place if there had not been a totally unnecessary kink set into this straight.

This all happened in about 1959 and Archie Scott Brown, who had one complete right arm and the other one had no fingers on it, but in spite of his handicap (or because of it), put on the most incredible performance seen anywhere in the world. He was later to die at Spa, Lister's greatest driver, but now he passed Moss broadside up at Fordwater. Baxter said: "This is impossible, it cannot be done, it can't be done. I can't believe Scott Brown is....". There was a stunned silence for several seconds. The audience, here on the bank, were listening absolutely with bated breath and then a sigh of relief from this very well known commentator, Raymond Baxter. "He's done it, I can't believe he's actually ... he's done it ... he's done it, he's passed Moss ... he's still there and he's now going through the 'S's". We all absolutely cracked up. It was a most incredible achievement.

Moss, the ultimate, the Aston Martin - of course a match for the Lister. The Lister's only benefit was that they were allowed to exceed the 3-litre engine limit, so Lister had installed the Jaguar 3.8. Quite a bit of power advantage, enabling this amazing feat to be done and Scott Brown did just pip him over the line by 1 or 2 lengths. I would not have believed such a thing possible had I not seen it, right here, with my own eyes. That was one of those legendary days that belong to Goodwood.

Subsequently I was to graduate through the Jim Russell Racing Drivers School, get my six signatures and International driver's license. I drove Formula Junior Lotus 22 for a couple of years. Didn't like it much. Got the Porsche 904 in 1964, which I destroyed here, but it was restored quickly with a new chassis. It was fibreglassed together and went out into the big wide world. We went to the 12-hour at Rheims and, with Paul Hawkins, won our Class there easily. Made the fastest time. Went to the Nürburgring, went to Spa. All 1000 kilometres, legendary places one only reads about. I think that John Surtees drove the best I have ever seen on a track at that Rheims 12-hour.

Having got out of Goodwood, revisiting today, you're very much back into the drudgery of life. You can see the horse racetrack now done up in tents, rather like Denver's International Airport or a miniature version. That's on top of the hill, but horse racing was not my mark.

At one point we had a charming little woman who was a housekeeper, Sussex born and bred, called Pearl Smith. She could neither read nor write and obviously couldn't drive a car. She had failed her driving test about 30 times at this stage. She was considered one of the leading contenders in Britain for this undistinguished title.

Wally Ward promoting the Jim Russell Racing Drivers School

I came here many times for practice sessions, races, etc and out of the corner of my eye I saw that Goodwood's horseracing track had a huge car park and thought, you know, this is where I could teach Mrs Smith to drive. She can't hit anything, but I'll make her go round all the lines, park in all the little parking slots, make her go back-wards and forwards, do all these elementary things, again and again and so we did. We did twenty or thirty sessions of this until she could stand it no more. She was a game old girl, a true Sussex peasant but strong as a horse. She passed her next test so that certainly impressed Mother and the locals. I got that idea on my bank that overlooks the Chicane. It looks actually due north I suppose.

Today they have little planes coming in on a cross runway every few minutes and the place is a hive of activity. They're about to build some other kind of marquee on top of what I term, my bank, but my memories take us back, back to the '50s in fact. I must have started thinking about being a racing driver in the year 1952 or 53 and I must have come here. It was Major Barker Bennett who first had the inspiration to bring me. We watched a very young Stirling Moss, driving the C-type Jaguar, nearly win in the heavy rain. Anyway, never forgot it. I suppose a spark was lit. Something started from here on in. Reg Parnell won that day, an older driver in the DBS-3 Aston Martin which was faster.

Actually it must have been pre-'52 or '53 because in '55 was the world's greatest accident at Le Mans. The war between Jaguar and Mercedes Benz. Hawthorn was driving the second-placed Jaguar at the time. 84 people were killed and a further 120 were injured at this terrible event. That was a D-type.

Today is motorbike day, which is rather nice. These amazing machines that you see now. Grand Prix cars look really more like a missile, I wouldn't even say an aeroplane. Aeroplanes are not that ugly, but motorbikes are magnificent. You can see the people that ride them, you can see the ventilated disc brakes and all the very sophisticated materials used. We're looking at a lovely, fairly small Yamaha here, a multi cylinder job with a huge silencer. That's the only condition at Goodwood today; you have to have an enormous silencer. It's chain driven; quite a beautiful looking thing. I could be very tempted. I think this young lady, she's got all her leathers on, is about to leap onto this thing and go screaming off into the blue... All these people look deliriously happy. It's still a world of total escape. You do this because you want to.

Here's an old Cortina, which has appeared from nowhere, Number 55. It was the first of the Cosworth Cortinas to appear on the track. I've got in with the bikers now. This quite aggressive young man with a broken thumb came up earlier and asked me if he could help, but I think he was worried I was snooping or doing something that I shouldn't be doing. Anyway, they seem to be quite happy now so we can wander the pits. In my day Goodwood had no pits. This mess was good old-fashioned painter's scaffolding and planks. I mean it was appalling.

There was the day that it even burnt to the ground. It was one of the TT's famous 3-hour races. Salvadori came in on the leading Aston Martin DBR1-300. It had pneumatic jacks so the pit stop was reckoned, full tank and tyres, to take 30 seconds. The pneumatic jacks kicked the car into the air and sparks flew out from the tail pipe of this very highly tuned six cylinder engine, the fuel churn was being chucked into the 30 gallon tank.

Well this lot exploded in about two seconds. Salvadori, like a fish (a long lanky fellow) leapt out and rolled onto the grass, by which stage his entire pit was on fire. No smoke, just flames. The fuelling churn... the tyres... the next car... and a few seconds later, the next two pits. All of Aston's pit was on fire. Goodwood, of course, only had buckets of sand with which to remedy this rather difficult situation and within another few minutes the entire pits were on fire. So now, Ferrari, Aston, Jaguar, everybody was walking out onto the pit apron with a pit signal saying *do not pit* and the driver would look cautiously to his right to realise that the entire wood scaffolding, with all its fuelling rigs, was completely ablaze.

I was on the opposite side of the road on that occasion with my cousin, Stella, and her husband, Michael. We were in some particular BARC enclosure I think. I'm now looking at a sign saying 'Chrysler'. That's where we were. You had to be on the other side to witness this incredible spectacle. Anyhow, all the pits burned to the ground.

Porsche were the most interesting to watch. Being small cars they were at the back of the pit section and the famous Huschke von Hanstein, who I was briefly later to drive for, walked out. He was a great character. He used to look like an English huntsman, without the hunting cap. He had a sports cap on but otherwise glasses, riding boots and hunter's raincoat, the perfect equipment for fox hunting. An incredible character with his rather thick-lensed glasses. He marched out into the pit apron and made various signals to his drivers, Bonnier and others, Edgar Barth (must have been), probably Porsche's best. "Do not come near the pits, if you've run out of gas, too bad".

It's all on fire at this stage, every one of them. Most incredible, by now they had got fire engines from Chichester and after half an hour the whole thing was extinguished. The scaffolding had melted and pit stops were sort of permissible, but rather a dangerous undertaking if you actually were able to collect any fuel at all.

Ferrari was there in big force with Hawthorn, Collins and Luigi Musso, people I had only read about in books really. To see all this under your nose 12 miles from mother's home was something for me to write home about to put it mildly. Winner of the day was, of course, Moss. There were three Astons. One burned to the ground, the second one, I think, also burned to the ground so the third one would have been driven by, probably, Jack Fairman. With half an hour remaining, the inevitable, the reason we all came to Goodwood - to watch the incredible Stirling Moss.

The Cortina has just gone past us at a very leisurely pace, but things have got so much faster. "Speed", as Paddy Driver used to say, "is relative".

The remaining Aston was brought into what was left of the pits, had some fuel put in it, I think, anyway Moss was put in the driver's seat. He was not amused, but of course realised that there was only one chance so in he climbs. The Ferrari at this point, with Hawthorn at the wheel, was pretty much in the lead but it's a much bigger, clumsier sort of a car really. So off goes Moss and of course we are riveted to see the maestro perform. He does and beats the Ferrari over the line by a few seconds. I mean there's nothing that any human being, not even Ferrari, can do to prevent such a thing from taking place. So that was the TT of Goodwood.

I had the MGTF 1500 at the time, so I think it must have been '58. Salvadori was to win Aston's only victory at Le Mans the next year, he and Carroll Shelby. Aston was not particularly renowned for its endurance. It had the speed, it had the handling but as a finisher it was one of the worst. So for Salvo, as he was called, and Carroll Shelby in '59 this was the lone Aston's greatest victory of all times. They actually outperformed the entire field. There were Ferrari's, Maserati's, you name it, all; so an incredible victory for the Aston DBR1-300. It had been out for about 2 years at that time so was old by racing standards.

The Cortina goes bombing by again, which reminds us that four wheels are still here. John Surtees came out with a most amazing statement, actually at this very place. Raymond Baxter asked him, because he'd made the transition very impressively from 2 wheels to 4 at that stage (later on Mike Hailwood, the greatest motorcycle racer of all time also made it). "Well John", Raymond asked: "what's the difference between 2 wheels and 4 wheels?" Being a very dry sort of character, John Surtees just said "2 wheels". That was the answer. A few seconds of silence and then Baxter went on to some other roving point, but it really was funny.

Looking due south to the beaches, Chichester is slightly to our right. They've now built a skidpan and go-kart circuit which all looks rather fun. They've got a timer's nest here, a sort of little clock tower. It has actually never looked so grand in its life before. Here we are now in the year 2000, but of course it can never be a Grand Prix track the road is still too narrow. There's only about 10 feet of grass verge on the outside and on the inside almost nothing at all so it does not conform in any way to a Formula 1 Grand Prix circuit or even a circuit where International races can be held, so these are now all sorts of privately sponsored races, just privateers really, keeping the flag waving as it were. There are lots of planes here, all parked. This one is a nice old Cessna 310, the likes of which I have flown in Cape Town and lots of little singles.

My plane in Cape Town, a Beechcraft Twin Bonanza painted in Lola's colours

The windsock indicates that the wind is blowing from the southwest. At some point we ought to be able to see the amazing Cathedral spire of Chichester, which is as sharp as the most sharpened pencil that has just been through the process. For some reason, things have grown (the trees, grass etc.) and I can't see it any more, the spire has gone. This is a unique little place because it is so special in its own quaint way. So many people have become involved in restoring it and building up the little airport. Its proximity is so grand, it is only 2 miles from Chichester, 8 miles from Midhurst and 50 miles out of London. Almost a pity that they didn't continue to modify it and keep it to Grand Prix specs, but well it's too late now, the road is far too narrow. It's still 2.4 miles, but it's a driver's bloody circuit.

Watching the Cortina going round again reminds me of another occasion with Porsche. I had about two years with Porsche on and off, the main being in 1966 when this very revolutionary, gull winged door 906 came along. This was supposed to be a semi works effort with AFN, which stood for Aldington Fraser-Nash, and myself being the driver. There were two cars. We each pooled in a certain amount of money and so we came down here. It never worked very well, this arrangement between Aldington and myself. There were many clashes of personality. I was more interested in reaching the top and they were more interested in winning races the easy way, going to places where the competition wasn't so fierce. Obviously, they got their way.

Our debut was at Castle Combe, which they owned, down near Bath. There was a local Champion there, a guy called Ron Fry, in a beautifully prepared Ferrari LM, which was completely outclassed by our Zeppelin looking 906. So that was a win, but not what I would have called a win. I would have liked, and wanted very much, to come here to take on the new Dino Ferrari driven by Mike Parkes. There were one or two others, but I don't think it was the 906 that excelled.

Always some serious competition here at Goodwood. We came here just weeks later to do some testing. I'm trying to remember the name of the right-hander after the pits, Madgwick Corner, anyway I lost it. This bloody little thing didn't handle, it had far too large a steering wheel. Amazing, when I say a driver's circuit, on every part of this place you have got to be extremely good. Like it or not this horrible little right-hander has two apexes in it and I think we'd survived the first one, but got it wrong on the second. Spun the little car, got it sideways and around came this unfortunate new, young Formula 2 ace called Roger Mac in The Chequered Flag Formula 2. He saw the road totally blocked off so went straight on and ploughed into the bank beyond, which I'm looking at right now. Quite a nasty shunt.

I opened the very flimsy gull wing door, feeling totally responsible for this unpleasant accident and got him out of the car, wheels still spinning, and shoved the ignition off.

There was no possibility of a fire, his bones were unbroken. He was shaken up and he didn't make a lot of sense so I inserted him into the spare seat of my 906 (a two seater) and drove him at fairly high speed back to the pits. Well now, of course, we have an audience and The Chequered Flag's, Graham Warner; so I, in true sporting fashion, duly apologised considering it all to be my fault.

Open test days do more damage than a motor race because the track is supervised by a manager who will open and close the gates; but that was it, no ambulance, no flag marshals, police or what have you. So, if you have a big shunt or set the pits on fire again, as Salvadori did, I mean that is it, it's at your own risk.

Mac was taken off to Chichester Hospital, which is only minutes away. Before this mishap Roger Mac, a very promising young man who had done some quite good races (even driving an E-type), was making his way in Formula 2, which was the prelude to Grand Prix racing big time. He was doing extremely well, but after that rather ugly shunt straight into the earth bank (with not nearly the same velocity that Stirling Moss had) he was never the same again. He did one or two races rather badly and was never heard of again.

All this of course, the reminiscing of Goodwood and my involvement in motor racing, took place over a period of 10 years exactly from 1960 till 1970, when I settled in Cape Town and married a Cape Town lady a year later.

This was another of my very bad judgements. If I'd stayed motor racing I'd have been better off. I'd have been safer somehow! So it's kind of fun in the Year 2000 to come back to this lot and to see all the trees grown, which didn't exist in my day, into now a lovely avenue of what appear to be small poplars on the outside of the circuit, leading all the way to Chichester. It's the road, which you actually can't see when you're on it, that will take you the back route right into Chichester.

I am looking at the city now but there has been a lot of growth here over the years since the days of the 60s. I can't see the Cathedral spire anywhere and the whole place is now a hive of activity with the little planes landing and taking off and the bikers flat out on the track. Such a different, whole other way of life really. Gorgeous view of the bikes going round Fordwater as they suddenly appear. I'd forgotten but, of course, this thing is called the Lavant so on my left, I'm trying to remember, is Roger Mac's corner, then you go on by the poplars, where the road actually dips. They've made every foot of this track as difficult (and as complicated) as is humanly possible and that is a feature in my ten years of racing.

Aged around 5 and a half, Bermuda

I can honestly say I've never driven on a track as difficult as this one. It took me years to beat, from being a spectator to coming here years later with Frank Gardner for the last five fairly serious ventures with the Lolas, then called the Grand Bahama Racing Car Company.

During my early years Mother and I lived at The Plaza in New York. I can still see the funny turret windows where she had her rooms, her suite for God knows how many weeks or months, but it seemed permanent to me. I was five, so that's how far my memory box goes back. My earliest memories are of being taken to Central Park for walks with Nanza, my nanny. We then lived in Lisbon for a while and aged about 6 we moved to Bermuda to Spanish Point,

750 miles from New York and a lot more from Goodwood, south east on the northwest shore of Bermuda. What's rather interesting for me about Bermuda, and I keep coming back to it over and over again, is that it's Portuguese so when we first lived here we were surrounded by Portuguese.

There was the taxi driver at the bottom of the garden, Mr Corday, who was married to a Jamaican lady called Gladys, who used to work for us as a domestic. They had of course a drove of children, 15 at least, but it had been nice to go to school with them all. Varying shades of café au lait, all good Roman Catholics (as indeed I was) and we all bundled into his taxi each school morning and off we went to St. Theresa's School in Hamilton.

We continue my story at the very northwest point of Spanish Point. It's a unique little peninsula because it touches the very end of the Royal Naval Dockyard where the municipal prison is. Standing here looking at the North Atlantic, it's clean and full of marine life, coral and flowers in various forms of Mediterranean-type, but more attractive than anything on the Cote d'Azur or certainly anywhere I've seen on the coast of Italy, or Europe. This has got a rustic charm. It goes back thousands of years, you can see it and wild things grow here. People paddling on the beach, some of them naked, some not. Nobody seems to care much.

Of course the US tourists glide past and there are signs everywhere saying, 'Positively no riding, no bikes'. Mine's left in the municipal car park, now half a mile away behind us.

It's such an incredible mix Bermuda, all the very best that you can get out of the US and the UK. It has English law, it has English police, it has an English government, but it has American telephones, American electricity and American plumbing. An absolute combo of the very best that you could suck out of these two extraordinary, similar and yet very diverse cultures. Tomorrow I shall go across to the dockyard. We start at Somerset, Long Bay where mother and I used to stay quite a lot at Cambridge Beaches. Beautiful little cottages parade along what would almost look like a Caribbean beach, but this is still very much North Atlantic. It happens to be in the Gulf Stream of Mexico and therefore subjected to unnaturally strong, hot winds which would otherwise make this a much cooler, almost English-type, climate than the one which it is, virtually subtropical.

Somerset is the County and village that we head for tomorrow. It's so odd that in this extraordinary structure of islands at Spanish Point, I am no more than one or two miles from the Royal Naval Dockyard yet, because I have to go all the way back through the City of Hamilton and around Riddles Bay, which is where we used to live at Little Sound, I have

24

made a complete U-turn slightly down to the top so the two, at this point where I sit now, almost touch but yet couldn't be further apart.

There is a space and a safety here, which I think is almost unique to anywhere in the world. It looks like almost no crime has ever been committed on this funny little island and yet I'm told the jail is full, but it's a fairly small jail. What's more significant about it is the Portuguese architecture all around us and, in particular, the City Hall. It has got two sort of mosque structures abutting a large Portuguese Colonial style building in the middle. You become aware that if Sir George Somers got here first, the Portuguese weren't very far behind. They left their mark on this island in much more lasting ways than the British did and somehow when you start digging, which is what I am doing, I feel a kinship with the Portuguese.

We first briefly lived in Lisbon before we came to Bermuda so Portuguese was probably the first language, or partly, that I learned outside my English tongue. I communicate with these people very easily. They were very Catholic, awfully understanding, very kind and I had no difficulty in going to school on my own, aged four, in Lisbon and back, unaccompanied on a train. I suppose I was given the right money for the fare, they seemed to know how much it was, probably a penny or an Escudo equivalent of it, and those same people are here at Spanish Point today.

I can see them and I can see the buildings and the architecture. It's got the same atmosphere; it's the poor part of Bermuda. The English looked down upon everybody who wasn't English or part English born and bred, so naturally on this island the Portuguese were looked upon as in the New Testament, the Samaritans, the absolute bottom of the pile. The inference being that nobody in his right mind would rescue an abandoned, or a derelict, lying beside the wayside.

In those days when you were robbed and beaten up you were cast off and left to your fate. Your time had come and anybody daring or mad enough to interfere with these forces of nature, fate or destiny could be almost guaranteed an untimely end. Some of that is also true with the implications and inference of the Good Samaritan. Luke 10:30.

My map is being blown about at this particular point, but it is the only way I can seem to try and gather my thoughts as to why we're actually here and what it is I want to actually say to you all about living here with my late mother and our old Irish nanny, Dot, from Dublin. Talk about an unlikely combination! Straight out of a 1960 Giles cartoon. Mother, always referring to herself as Vera, thin as a coat hanger, strapped with milk bottles and medicine all around her and old Nanza, always dressed in a black hat, black coat, black shoes, black stockings and a large bun with a hairpin holding her hat on.

This apparition was to be seen right here in the Portuguese part of Bermuda. What they must have made of us, I know not, but I know that I could relate to these people straight away and they to me. It's funny how a chemistry happens between certain people or groups of people. No matter how much you bend the rules, or accommodate, the chemistry works for us. It's like a light switch, it's on or it's off. So my chemistry worked here. Obviously the visual beauty is always stunning. Bermuda over all these years.

I'm 58 as I write this book so I've been coming here for a bit more than 50 years now. That's what I can go back to and I can honestly sit here, right now, and say that it has hardly changed a bit. Over this period of time, England I can hardly recognise any more. The odd little bit is untouched, like Arundel Castle, but all routes to Brighton shall we say and Bognor Regis, well I could be in a foreign country. Even the people are completely foreign. Here, almost nothing has changed and that's incredible and unique. They've kept the 20 mile an hour speed limit, they've kept one car per family, therefore the housewife who has to do the shopping and take kids to school nearly always gets to use the car while the husband, or men, go to work on buzz bikes. Everybody, much more than in Rome or Naples, zaps around on these funny little bikes, which make their own special sound and have their own peculiar smell, but lend a very charming individual character to this island.

Leaving Bermuda after Honeymoon no. 2

When you have looked at the sea and the sky and the clouds long enough in the gentle breeze, I start to become aware that that is it. The French would say c'est beau or c'est belle, but afterwards there is nothing else. There are two cinemas on the entire island and one theatre. For all its charm, both Nassau and Freeport and St Kitt's and Jamaica are rather like that. They're cultural wastelands.

You don't want to exercise your marbles too much in a place like this, which is the reason most people, and I have always noticed this in the Caribbean as well, drink like fish. Last days of Rome, mainly wine by the gallon. I find that a most disturbing business, which renders the subject completely and mentally incompetent to the point where they fall down and crash into trees or run the odd pedestrian over. It doesn't seem to cause any undue alarm, it's such a frequent occurrence; but if you're stone cold sober, and I try to be most of the time, you can't help but notice these strange inconsistencies in behaviour.

At Spanish Point, on the way to Admiralty House where I shall make my last little visit, we have Clarence Cove (or Deep Bay), which is where I took wife No. 2 on our honeymoon.
One of the most beautiful places I have ever been to and with another person.
If ever surroundings and atmosphere could have made a successful marriage, then Clarence Cove would have done it, but as you will see the very reverse was destined to happen.

The trees around here have been excavated into an extraordinary sort of square, dug into the coral and then soil added so that you've got this seven foot square and about four foot deep sunk hole, for want of a better word, into which grows this gorgeous fragrant Bermudan Cedar. It's been here a while so it's quite an old tree and beyond the rocks the ferry goes into the Royal Naval Dockyard from Hamilton itself no less.

On the rocks below we see some examples of the locals. We used to call them Mulattos in the early days, that is a mixture of Afro/Bermudan/ Jamaican/coffee au lait, but very pretty and very nice people. You can't call them black and you can't call them white, which is in a way a relief, but you sure can say they're Bermudans. All of these people, part European/ part African, are very much aware that they are the slaves who made it out of the south and somehow won their freedom.

We've come up upon the dry dock, more rusted through with more holes and more sunken than last year and yet, in its day, an incredible piece of engineering. To think that this thing was hauled all the way across the Atlantic from England by four HMS ships. It is really quite mind-boggling and of course it says on it, very English: *'Danger. Keep off!'* As if anybody in their right mind would presume to climb upon this poor old, dirty, forlorn, wrecked, degenerate hulk of scrap, which looks lethal with parts of it razor sharp.

From where I stand and I'm about 20 feet now due east of the hulk, but the sign is as clear as can be. It must be as old as the hulk itself, *'Danger, Keep Off'*! The tide always seems to be out. Nearly all these dear little boats, which I'm sure are Portuguese owned, are very small and rather humble but charming in their own way.

Clean, well kept and nicely maintained. They're all lying on their sides as they do in the Cornish fishing villages quite often. Every time I come here Spanish Point is always at low tide and these funny little boats are always keeled over. There's quite a posh mahogany one fairly far ahead and then the little Yacht Club and there we have it, Spanish Point.

I find this very hard to confront, even now, because this is where I brought wife No. 2 on our honeymoon. If ever external beauty or aesthetic powers had made a success of that marriage then this would have done it and yet there we were, on the second or third day of our honeymoon, like two people standing on opposite sides of a river, a small river, but neither one willing to make the slightest movement to cross. I, being I suppose of a chauvinist's generation, considered she had to make at least an overt gesture.

We had been forced into cover by quite a severe storm. I got the boat tied up, left it overnight and intended to go and get it the next morning before leaving the island. Somehow it was symbolic to honeymoon here but only symbolic of things that I had done in the past. It wasn't her choice, it really wasn't the place that had anything to do with her, but it was the idyllic honeymoon spot. We had a week. My friend, Kirk Kitson, lent me his little boat, which had two very nice outboard engines, and we went off to the Reef.

We stopped at islands, had picnics there and did this and that, all the things that honey-mooners would ideally like to do, but the honeymoon ended. It came to an explosive conclusion on the final day. We had been forced into cover by quite a severe storm. I got the boat tied up, left it overnight and intended to go and get it the next morning before leaving the Island.

Sandra insisted on going with me, a person who could neither swim nor see very well, who had no nautical knowledge or talent whatsoever, so to me she was a liability. This was the beginning of the American woman that I was about to see under the paint. They now dominate; the man is the second-class citizen here, one of my pet phobias, so Sandra laying down the law was showing her true colours and I was livid.

As we go down the path I'm coming right into this incredible little cove, which also overlooks at the far end, St George's, the oldest part of Bermuda. We make a little 'S' bend and into this cove a sandy, horseshoe bay cove and one of the most beautiful natural phenomena I have ever seen. It feels to me only yesterday that I drove that Boston Whaler in here with Sandra on board. By God I thought we had it made. Everything seemed right with the world.

It's so like motor racing, you find yourself out in the lead, you've done your homework, your practice, everything's gone reasonably well and you've had a little bit of luck. You're out in front and in control of the situation and to yourself everything seems fine, the picture keeps getting more positive and suddenly, bang something happens a blow out, a gear strip, a second away and you're not only dangling through the wayside, ploughing through the undergrowth missing concrete objects by inches but you are fighting for your bloody life, one second later.

We got Kitson's boat back and I sent her off shopping to get a teapot that I had particularly wanted, which we did not have at home whilst I did the packing. She came back having bought something else that she wanted, a teapot which was too small, didn't match the set, was totally inappropriate and with my money of course. I think it was then that I exploded.

I was vicious and regrettably so. It's an unattractive quality. We've all got this beast in our nature and it came out of me then and there. She was pretty shook up because the American woman's supposed to be worshipped, but not by me. I was meant to fit in, go to the clubs, become a member of respectable New York society, attend their bridge parties and do the posh things that New York City folk like to do.

Even living on Long Island, Oyster Bay, you're within half an hour or an hour's drive from all this, all those people spend fifty percent of their time in New York City and fifty percent on Long Island. Kitson mentioned it to me one evening when we were talking about members of the Grace side of my family. It could have been me talking, but he went straight to it: 'those that worship wealth above all things have nothing else' and this is true of Grace. It's true of a certain type, endemic on the North Shore of Long Island. I've been to a few parties out on the Island and those people are exactly the same, they come out of a stereotype mould.

When I stayed with the Oliver Graces in Oyster Bay Cove they did the rather gushy American thing, I would quantify that by saying 'Eastern American thing'. 'Oh, we must ring Margaret (mother) and tell her about the imminent wedding, the good news'. Margaret of course sternly and coldly addressed me on the phone. "Well, it sounds like a repeat performance". That's all she had to say and by God was she ever right. 11 years later and here I sit now another 15 years down the road, certainly not in the same predicament, but you talk about a hole-in-one, Cecily wife no.1 and Sandra wife no.2.

Sandra honestly thought I would become one of them and somehow this, even now I can talk about it, violates my every principle of integrity, honour and to some extent (it sounds hypocritical) but morality. I realised that this was not a marriage at all. I don't know what she's doing for the ride; maybe it's money but I don't think so. I think she thought that with me on board she was just going to have a good time, get what she wanted then and there and I would just write out the cheques. I would become, and I think Lollo (Lorraine) Grace thought so too, I would become a north-eastern, New England American. They really had another thing coming and that, I think, was my anger. It was directed at Sandra and somehow this last visit to Bermuda has exorcised that ghost. The woman was a fool, but are we not all sometimes? It's there, except she was a fool all the time.

I was now going to further my own ends, but I hadn't decided what they were. I knew that I had to do something quickly and very thoroughly, but I did it all wrong according to the local folklore. So I became the outcast when I set out to divorce Sandra. I broke all the rules here, I broke the New York rules and I broke the general American rules. I became the outcast, like Sarah Woodruff. We have relatives called Woodruff – very nice people, they're Grace cousins from New Zealand.

The experience of this second marriage, the divorce and the awful difficulties along the way told me that the time had come to completely restructure my life. Cape Town (where I had lived for many years) was thousands of miles away, where the way of life had changed, the beach had changed and my family (cousins) had all left. So 1981 was the time for me to actually uproot the stakes and move to New Jersey, as it happens. The world changes slightly when you get to New Jersey, the people are quite different. Lots of foreigners, as the locals call them, mainly Italian but, from where I lived within a radius of ten miles from Newark, almost every pop star of the 50s and 60s that you can think of comes from there. Sarah Vaughn, Connie Francis, Frankie Avalon, Gloria Gaynor, Dionne Warwick, obviously Frank Sinatra and Rick Nelson, so when I went across that GWB I went into a foreign country. Out of the bus you could see it straight away, it was like going from Holland, through Aachen into Belgium. The people were different, the dress, the style and everything about them. I knew at that point that if I am to survive, and my survival was indeed threatened, I've got to throw the past behind me in a big way and not only give Sandra a shove but my family as well.

When I moved over the bridge to New Jersey, the Grace's took that as a total rejection and now that I come to think of it, it was. With friends like that, who needs enemies? The phrase doesn't quite apply because they were, and still are, family; but having got me into such deep water I have to confess in my soul I regard them as enemies, even Lorraine. So I rejected her and I rejected the Graces, their values and their worship of wealth. Now that I'm years down the road the Long Island Grace's don't talk to me, nor I to them.

It's been five years and all the bridges have been burned between me and Long Island. It's only literally about five miles away at this point, but I feel estranged. I broke all the rules without intending to. It's sad about Lollo, my aunt, companion and often friend. I miss her a lot, but she has chosen to cut me dead and regrettably I see no way back. I don't really know, in her case, what I did wrong. Obviously the year-old marriage to Sandra and the five-year divorce is what upset the locals so I'm warming up as to why Lollo has cut me dead, but this second marriage I committed to at aged 40, hardly a kid out of school, but New Jersey now there's another thing.

Lollo mentioned when she came over to have a look at my place in New Jersey, even Oliver was around then. She said, "you've left us, you've gone away". It's only across the Hudson River for Christ's sake. It's a mile wide at this point, but she was right I have left them and put Sandra, them and that North Shore Gold Coast way of life behind me. Can't quite, or don't like having to, define why I despise those who worship wealth as a thing of fortune almost like a God, but I'm afraid that does typify W.R. Grace completely. Poor old Grace has been polluting the rivers of up-State New York for years. I knew all about all that. Poor old Grace, yes, but the fortune. 'The Civil Action' with John Travolta and upper New York State, that's my family.

I didn't choose them and I suppose they didn't choose me but at this point in time, by God, I have rejected them and they me. I guess I did it first, although I didn't do it in cold blood or even quite intentionally.

The Grace Building, slightly west of Citicorp. It's in fact three blocks west of Citicorp, between it is the GM Building which also the same height, all three are the same height. The GM Building has flats in it and looks rather like a perpendicular harmonica, an extraordinary looking building but quite attractive. When I look at the Plaza now, it is fourteen storeys high and fifteen windows, or blocks, across. It used to look a huge building to me but now the Grace Building looms above it, somewhat in disgrace. It's sad days and maybe the final days of W.R. Grace.

I don't know how they'll last after the civil action, but it's called No. 9 and it stands directly behind the Plaza. It's a ghastly looking slab of concrete and black glass, skirted by pre-cast, filled-in panels. Grace, I don't know, a sad, pathetic block. A blob from the past. I even feel guilty in rejection. Maybe they do too; maybe that's why Lollo has cut me off for five years. She knows what she stands for and what I certainly stand for and they don't have much in common at all.

The Grace Building, New York

'Civil Action' explains all that, as I look at the W.R. Grace Building with a measure of contempt. It may be a display of great wealth, it's one of the biggest skyscrapers in this City and it's family, but I have to say I am utterly ashamed of it. I was quite ashamed of it before Sandra, but having become intimate with the WASP (beautiful word that, it means white Anglo Saxon Protestant), she was not an individual of her own making, she was just the product of a totally degenerate society. She was one of them and she obviously, in her innocence and corruption, thought I would become one of them and Lorraine (Lollo) thought so too. I must say that it never occurred to me that they would expect such changes to take place. Now that I have been here for 15 years I realise that New Yorkers do expect you to become one of them, and being such a rugged individual I have made my statement.

In 2000, as I dictate this book I am, and have for 15 years been, the resident patient, the one from New Jersey where I am completely accepted. To that extent New York and New Jersey are incompatible. There are certain compositions or structures which will not switch. The Jerseyians will go home to Jersey; the New Yorkers will stay in New York. So I, unwittingly, rejected after Uncle Oliver's death, which was in mid-January of 1992, knew it would be the end. I was a bit shook up to find he dies within two weeks of the last Christmas we spent together, that was the last time I saw Oliver and Lorraine together.

I saw Lorraine a few times later but she had changed. She was deeply upset by his death, but I think I missed him and still miss him more than she. We were incredibly close, he was my uncle, actually not quite but he had been like an uncle to me all my life. He was a very kind, very understanding man, maybe the only one. As Mother had often said, "he's the only apple in the bunch, the rest are all rotten". Mother had a way of saying things, of oozing charm from every pore quite without equal, so I used to take it with a pinch of salt but occasionally she was absolutely bull's eye on target.

Oliver was the exception absolutely to the rule. He did nothing illegal that I know of. He might have tried it a bit, no more than myself, to see if he could get away with it. Oliver was every bit as good as I am, if not better, at testing the temperature and if the temperature wasn't quite right or if there was something out of place he wouldn't do it. Somehow I picked a lot of that up from him but also had a fair measure of, I think it's called intuition, myself. So mother had a way of saying things and in this particular case, subsequently post mortem and all that pollution, J. Peter Grace president of W.R. Grace being nearly bankrupt at this stage, she was absolutely right. Bull's eye in one. They, along with Beatrice Foods, which is the largest food corporation in this country, unbelievable we are talking billions here.

Beatrice got off because their lawyer was the slickest thing on two legs and Grace got all the blame. They were guilty and so was Beatrice but poor old Grace got shatter-bombed by everybody in sight. This is some 12 years ago but I'd seen it coming. I knew all this was going to take place. I don't know if that's intuition but you don't make these kind of bucks without skinning a few rats on the way. Poor old Grace got so big. America's oldest serving executive when he did a very good accounting job for President Reagan into government waste. He did such a good job that one of the companies put a contract out on him, so he had to leave town. Dear old Grace had to take off for Florida, Boca Raton. He's been in the ground a few years now, cancer got him but if the cancer hadn't got him I think the family would have, not my family but the Italian one. Did too good a job, to give him his due, for the Reagan administration. He accounted for millions that had been thrown away, wasted (actually billions) in favour of the government.

So we've come face to face, and it's always such a stark experience, with W.R. Grace. I look him in the face and I shudder, and I shuddered years and years before that, at this obnoxious, vulgar, ghastly, tasteless building. If you're going to spend billions on building an obelisk why not make it attractive.

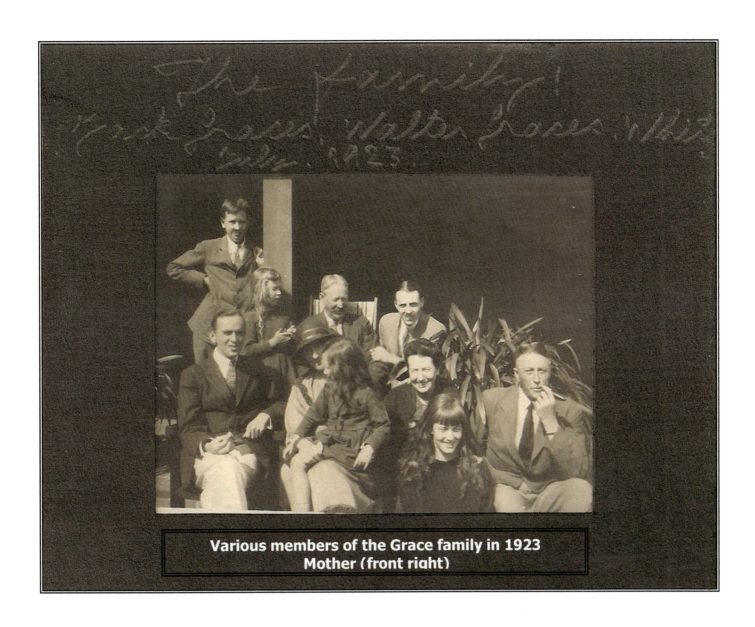

**Various members of the Grace family in 1923
Mother (front right)**

To it's left the GM Tower, which is also modern but quite attractive and terribly functional and you can see that it is and it's got inbuilt AC. I'm sure there's not a window that you can open, it has lots of slits but a very nice kind of glass that doesn't reflect. It's always sad to come back face to face with my family, Grace. No wonder, when we're not talking any more. I could see it and I obviously would rib Lollo about it. She's still got shares in the company I think, I'm sure she has. Yes, it's true I did tease Lollo unmercifully about the Grace episode.

Even Oliver had amassed an incredible sum of money, but he'd done it on his own and I must say I can't entirely blame him. Kitson called it 'mega-bucks'. I didn't notice in the obituary, because it mentioned a lot of other things that I thought as being of more importance, but I do know that, unlike W.R. Grace which was a third or fourth generation family corporation or company, Oliver was kicked out. As a stockbroker on his own he formed an alliance with Stirling Grace & Co. His partner, Stirling, died quite young. Oliver ran it himself terribly successfully, but very safe as houses. He took no risks. He died worth I think it was 80 million, which isn't bad from nothing! So when people talk, as Sandra did during the divorce, about 'he's heir to the Grace fortune', meaning me because my initials happen to be W.R. Grace, they think that in some subtle kind of way I'm Donald Trump II, but it's merely a coincidence that my initials are M.W.R. Grace de'Udy.

44

Sandra didn't know that and that was the joke of it. She thought she'd landed 'the big one' and as I said to the judge in Hackensack: 'if that were so, you're not getting it. You picked the wrong dude this time'. She cried. She boo-hooed like a baby. I was really surprised at that. She was licked, totally and utterly licked. That's what I wanted, but I can't say it gave me any satisfaction. It was rather sad really, if not sad, then pathetic.

I'm standing right on the very rock edge face now looking down about 80 feet, two inches too forward and down we would hit the rocks below. I parked the boat under here with Sandra, looking up at all this. Cave, after cave, after cave all natural coral phenomena. Just like yesterday for me. One always has a sort of a guilt complex. What did I do wrong? When I look at this place it doesn't appear that anybody could have done anything wrong, but somebody did. Was it me or was it her?

You know when you're alive when you're on a cliff edge looking down, which I am this minute thinking about these past things, walking a tightrope, but I wouldn't have done it any other way even with all the blood and the broken bones and God knows what. Still I can only think now I'm so pleased to come back. I even remember her with a degree of fondness, although I'd cheerfully string her up along the end of 20 feet of nylon clothesline and have her tread air for at least 30 seconds.

Short-lived satisfaction in all that kind of thing, I'm better off here thinking about these things and musing over them. I'd upset the locals, but what always bounces in my favour is living in New Jersey. Now I'm 58 I feel a bit older and I think we have got a lot more control, or leverage over our so-called destiny than I ever believed before. There is something that you can do about this and somehow in an indirect way I'm doing it now, I'm coming back yet again to another graveyard, but a very attractive one. I feel very peaceful, very happy and very much in control here. I've missed nothing.

A gorgeous sun is starting to go down and I can suddenly see over my shoulder a cruiser no less, quietly chugging its merry way along towards the West. It's got very small guns on the foredeck. It may be American, can't see any flags. It could be British, it's so small and it's got quite a large gun with a turret/tower at the front, but it's not mean enough or sharp enough like a Formula 1 car to look like a destroyer, so its got to be a cruiser. I'm beginning to see the number on the side of this thing. When it's American the letters and numbers are in a sort of black and white 3D code, yes she's flying the Stars and Stripes so she is a Yank. The Americans used to have a naval base in our day when we lived here, quite an effective one so I think they still keep some of it going and they have free docking rights. I have never ever seen a British warship here in years, not a minesweeper, not a cruiser and certainly not a battleship. The Royal Navy, should we say, don't seem to be in any control of this part of the North Atlantic at all now, it's all US. The cruiser really is cruising to put it mildly, very slowly. I could walk faster. What a little treasure this place is, absolutely surrounded by the most incredible fauna and flora. It's still one of the best beauty spots anywhere I have ever been to. As we take these long steps up, it's very like the paths to Villa La Cava, mother's villa in Cannes.

Villa la Cava An artificial grotto sheltering a spring picked from the brook of Les Gabres at the bottom of garden is at the origin of the name of this property situated on the California Hill. However, one is startled by a brick gloriette of Moorish inspiration with its painted and laid in blue ceramics dome in the surrounding area of an English style villa. An artefact built in a landscape garden designed on a down slope plot and containing several rustic staircases framed with rockeries leading to a water pool supplied by a beautiful cascade. Constructed in 1868 for M. de Wesselow, a British citizen, in the style of the English cottages, high attic roofing with spiked windows covers the Villa La Cava. The building dominates the garden planted of rare species. Walter H. Grace from New York buys the property in 1923. He probably added the wing on the ground floor. After his death in 1932, his widow Alice asks the American architect Barry Diercks established in Théoule, to heighten this wing by one level. In 1952, Mrs. De'Udy, the new owner, divides the garden into several independent plots, today constructed, and the house into apartments, while keeping the distinctive aspect of the original construction. It seems that the grotto has been preserved.

The minaret over the garage at Villa La Cava, inside the garage was the stalactite cave from which the Villa got its name.

There are hibiscus, some oleander, lots of palms of different kinds, completely sheltered and yet it faces northwest exactly, so if I wanted to go back to New York I just have to face the way I am, climb on a jet plane and 730 miles later I would land at Newark surrounded by gas, scrap metal, pollution, garbage and all the other delightful things that go along with New Jersey.

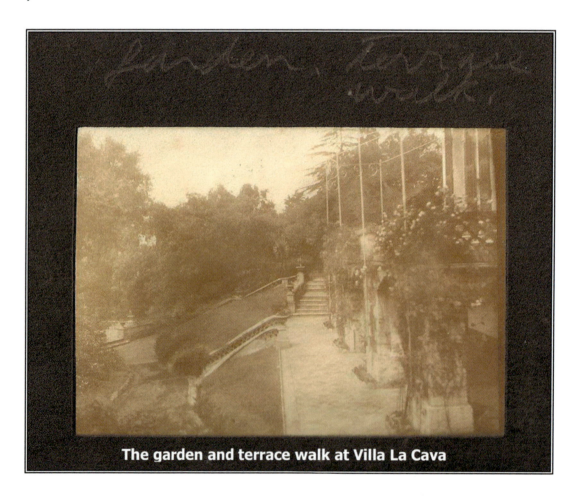

The garden and terrace walk at Villa La Cava

Villa La Cava, entrance and new car in 1926

Frank Gardner's big win at Thruxton in the Lola in 1969 where we actually beat Sid Taylor's Lola, with Denny Hulme driving. Ron Bennett (in red suit) was the best Lola mechanic of all time.

So this Grand Bahama Racing Car Company came to Goodwood to do it's testing. All our engines came from TRACO. Roger Penske introduced me to them, TRACO, my first two engines, Travers and Coon. This was all actually very big time stuff. Gardner was testing a peculiar sports car called the Ford F3L, which was an enclosed Formula 1 car. It never did take off but it was an interesting idea, which Mercedes had done some years before, to enclose the open wheels, streamline (or aerodynamicise) a Formula 1 car to see if it would go any quicker.

Frank was testing this F3L, but he made me do all the bloody slogging with this Lola. Bedding in the brakes, scrubbing new tyres, trying out different shock absorbers and coil springs, but it got me over my innate dread and fear of Goodwood which I'd had all the time since that day Stirling Moss damn nearly killed himself. I was sort of psychologically in shock. I remember watching my mirror being obliterated on my bloody doorstep by this rather insignificant little track. How could it happen? Well, after hundreds of miles I got over this anger, or fear, and the peculiar mix of emotions I had against Goodwood.

As the bikes go by I begin to realise that I have become really professional in my old age. I was 30 then, it was about 1970, or 69.   I knew every inch of this track, I had to and Gardner made me. He would go by in his F3L as and when he wanted to, but he just said: "Don't look for me, I'll get around somehow" in his drawling Sydney Australian accent.

Anyhow, Gardner left me alone, left me to get on with it. We weren't doing fast laps, but it made me study every inch of this circuit, where Moss went off, how the accident happened and where Maston Gregory broke his leg on the S-bend just before the Lavant Straight. There's another, but I've forgotten most of the names of these places although I suppose they'll come back. At least you can see the spire from here, with poplar trees lining the place. My Uncle Ron is buried only a few miles from here.

There's so much personal history attached to this place for me. It's where the motor racing began and where I'm trying to write about it, trying just to touch upon what happened. This was obviously the place to be and certainly where it ends.

Turning the clock back 50 years, the first place we stayed at when we came back from Bermuda was the boarding house section at Iping House. This was Lady Hamilton's house, bought for her by Horatio Nelson while he served as Admiral in Portsmouth. It very definitely is haunted, I think, by Emma Hamilton who also happens to be this relative of mine by marriage to one of the Grevilles. I found all their portraits hanging in Cawdor Castle, which is outside Inverness and which also happens to be the ancestral home of a distant relative (Campbell), who much to my horror sided with the English at Culloden against the Highlanders, so here now we're at the beginning of Emma Hamilton's walk.

Cobblestone paving, at least two Centuries old and the wall marking the boundary of Iping House, a section of which was the boarding house and really my first conscious memories as a young, impressionable lad. I must have been eight or nine, so that gives me the fifty-year bracket.

To see all this again now after America, the air conditioning, chewing gum, milkshakes. Centuries old, Iping House itself and crawling with history. Going back to the Norman Conquest this is one of the first places where the Conqueror built one of his many chapels which he built all over the place. He must have been a fanatic, but he did a good job as they're still here to this day. We've just climbed, not quite cobblestones but very neatly laid slabs of slate and very finely interwoven stones right to the edge of the gate of Iping House. The boarding house section, which must have been an addition, has completely disappeared. Nobody quite knows what happened to it, some people think it fell on the fleur-de-lis gates here, so now you have the French influence in the middle of West Sussex.

Straight ahead and down the drive and we're looking right at the front of Iping House with its original front door, a few arched windows to the side and then two arched windows above. The period of the door is certainly right, I don't think they've altered the brickwork much and there's a largish window above the door and that's the sum total of Iping House. It's actually quite small, but nice enough for her and after all he was not a wealthy man I don't think. This is the edge that was haunted. Mother said so and I'm sure she was right. The Iping boarding house led into the edge of this and we stayed in this edge, I remember that.

She must have been fascinated. She'd listen to the river, which at this point winds down just like our section of it at Chithurst, which is a mile up river, two miles actually. Here it's shallow but it doesn't flow like it does at Stedham. Looks decidedly awkward and uncomfortable and gets blotted out and of course that's naturally so because it's been through the mill.

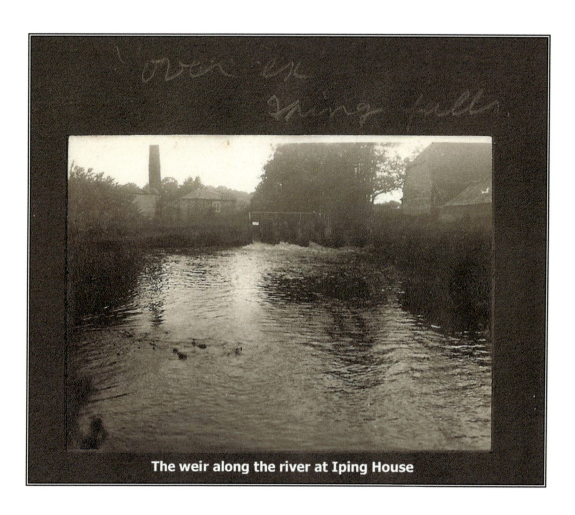

The weir along the river at Iping House

Here it's the bit of the Rother with actually goes and assumes its natural course having been and truly interfered with by the Mill. I suppose that's what mills are for. The other side of the mill used to be ours but not any more, that's long gone. Gone with the wind. Gone with history.

It's quite a small building, but very historic and absolutely full of character. It's easy to peel off a Century or two here with no trouble at all. It comes off in seconds. Coachman's Cottage, it looks as if you've got three or four Centuries since its construction, it's of that ilk. Row upon row of restored ex-workmen's cottages, all with TV aerials. Now restored, they're millionaire's nests.

The beginning of the kitchen garden is on the right. What amazing soil this must be and then on to the gate with its charming old lock. You're expected to look after all this yourself and people do, they always have, but now we're into the Park, Emma Hamilton's Park. She would have walked along here thinking thoughts, close to nature. Beautiful trees, I think they must be chestnuts. The silence is so evasive, a few thousand miles from Central Park and yet still a park somehow. It would have once been Iping Park at least three Centuries ago, but today on this dry and parched path there's not much of England's green and pleasant land here.

It's been a baking summer, 100 degrees in New York and 90 degrees here. It must be about 80 or 85 degrees now, it sure feels like it. Everywhere looked burnt as we came in on Virgin's 002 this morning over Bromley in Kent, made a U-turn and went back on ourselves to the airport. Couldn't get a slot so the poor pilot had to plough out to Reading, gradually climbing again.

What a mess, but we eventually made another U-turn, the pilot got his slot and we did have a most spectacular entry right over Windsor Castle. Here, in the beginning of the forest, violent voices and eyes all look on wondering, listening, watching. In doing this I hope to unravel these faraway places that are all intrinsically linked by memory. How many ghosts are there here today? There are a few I can mention and one or two I can't, but I find I am almost duty-bound to revisit these places, retrace the footsteps, to see where I have been after so long and after such a mileage. The thing that makes an enormous difference here is that I am not the same person and I have great difficulty in deciding who this person now is. It's almost several lives that have been led in the past to now getting here.

For one, the ghost of Gerald Oversby. I am quite certain he's now on the other side. How, or why, I know not, but I bet I could make a shrewd guess, probably a motor accident. He drove like a fool, like Madox and Geoffrey Clifton in "The English Patient".

There's a horse on my right, which believe it or not looks totally green; as green as the trees behind it, only you would think I was hallucinating. I mean it's as hot as Hades out here and this unfortunate horse has got a coat on it, hence the colour I think, or am I seeing things? Jetlag does some quite unpleasant things to the mind and we're only a few hours on this English soil. The horse himself was at one stage black, or slightly off black and he is coming over to have a look. It's got the name 'Rambo' on his coat, Ireland, Horse Wear of Ireland. Very nicely done, beautifully strapped, actually he's a sort of dapple. Now we've had a closer look at him, what a disguise. He's a sort of a dapple-grey although he has got a black face. Quite a smart pony of about fourteen hands, rather similar, maybe slightly larger, to Bonnie, my old pony.

Uppark was where Emma Hamilton's mother worked. Somehow she engineered, or got a meeting to come about with Horatio Nelson, who was quite a frequent visitor to Uppark in those days fairly shortly before he fell at Trafalgar. That must have been the end of her and certainly it was the end of him. So on she trotted, maybe to Scotland, which may be why the portrait of her hangs next to Lord Greville in Cawdor Castle. Next to it is yet another relative, her name keeps cropping up in the Grace anecdotes over and over again, if not Greville it's almost something like Hamilton-Carr.

Same show jumps were here last year on my visit, and the year before. Busy gymkhana-type people these, with lots of ponies. This is horse country all right, not racing, but more show jumping, quite a lot of hunting and of course gymkhanas where I began to ride as well. Did all those funny bends, bobbing, looping and ups and downs. It made one good in the saddle and certainly had variety. Lots of horse hooves about our feet.

 I wonder if they were like that then for Emma Hamilton? Probably not. She may have had some influence in them days around the locals and yet the English were such prudes. Poor lady was probably looked down upon, like the French Lieutenant's whore. She must have walked this way many, many times. Probably not a very happy lady, after all the mistress's life can't be much fun. Must be very insecure. He, at least, did his best to make her feel needed and secure, but she was nothing more than a mistress, a sort of a plaything. It's not the same as being a lawfully wedded wife. I think he did have one, but her part here at Iping, was to be his mistress and to be available and at home for him whenever he was allowed shore leave, which was probably not very often. At the end of the day when all's said and done, when you're alone, then what do you think? Who are you? What are you? Where are you?

If anyone haunts Iping House then it is she. She has the right, if anybody has the right. These haunting souls linger on in places, I remember mother saying so. It definitely seems women are more psychic than men. I can attest to that. I don't think I'm psychic, I've never seen; but I sure can feel it and I have a sense of awareness. Mother had a much keener developed sight. She must have been aware of an afterlife, though she wasn't very sure what form it took, but she was aware of the spirits, of the people that haunt and she was particularly aware of this one. She drew my attention to it early on; I must have been aged eight. I think it was just before I went to Worth, near Crawley and East Grinstead, when we stayed here.

I remember, I suppose I was always fearless, that she pointed out to me that this place was haunted, without question. I could see that, seeing wasn't quite what I mean to convey, but I could feel it. So if the Hamilton ghost lingers here, it haunts this place or is it the other way round, that the spirit cannot be released and that it's somehow tied to this place. Is that what a ghost is? A form that is somehow bound by forces beyond its control.

The side of the house is almost by the river on the left of the bridge, with the same area at the front so that makes it pretty square. It looks small but actually if you take it as a square it's quite big.

Inside it probably is. It's no great 'To the Manor Born', like Audrey Forbes-Hamilton, but it's certainly happy enough. It's more than a country cottage, very much more, Iping House. There's a pink rose to one side of the house, I think we did stay in this section some fifty years past which seems to me like an incredible length of time ago. I can't imagine as a young person even living that long, seeing all the risks that have been taken. Imagine living fifty years, but here we are.

Iping House is now behind us and to the right above us two huge oaks, really big ones. I know this one's been here all of my lifetime and much more. We've done the full lap of public footpath, Emma Hamilton and Iping are now behind us and facing due west is a fairly cloudy, grey sky; it could even bear rain. There is security in things that don't change. To come back after fifty years and find the same tree, the same sign and the same manhole in the same place, that's security. It can also be boring, but at least it's stable. I am on a private drive, Iping House, Coachman's Cottage, the Pheasantry and the Vinery, wouldn't you know. Who needs one?

Our walk takes us down to the level of the brown and parched wheat field. It looks quite a sorry sight and I haven't seen it like this for some years. We're in a bit of a valley here, Iping, next to Chithurst, Chithurst-le-Trotton.

We've now reached the Rother River, or what's left of it. It seems smaller and shallower than I remember, but maybe it's not. It's a funny little winding river from somewhere near Petersfield, which is why the Petersfield Angling Club had the fishing rights to our three miles, or mother's three miles, of river that ended her section at Iping. There, it is a gorgeous little river to kayak down. That's what my uncle, Cleve Grace, did often. He was a renowned eccentric but he certainly had the right idea.

The water level is actually quite normal here, rather beautiful. It's also a bit cooler under the trees in the shade by the river. Tirra Lirra by the river, across from us they're baling right now. This is the time, but they'll only just make it as this stuff is baked or nearly roasted. The tractor in front of us is going apace, piling it up. When they do work, they work very fast these people particularly when it's a broiler like this one. Let's see we're the 2nd of August, definitely the right side of the pond if it is a

The Rother near Emma Hamilton's Walk

roaster like this. This lot has already been baled so they belt it up just in case it rains. I remember it from mother's old farm at Chithurst, just two and a half miles from here where we lived after Iping. If it rained overnight the entire crop could be destroyed in a day.

I learned to plough some of the fields myself in the autumn under Major Hope, who taught me to drive the tractor. Had to drive well to plough. They want those furrows straight as a dye. Major Hope was our bailiff who had tried in vain to talk me into being interested in becoming a gentleman farmer; the very word gave me the shudders. Unfortunately I can't bear dealing with this stuff, it's pretty, it's quaint and it's incredibly free, but that's about it. I mean this is like the climax of the whole year; this is the big deal, the pay-off. Harvest time, great excitement and then that's it, nothing happens. You are almost enslaved into watching television in the evenings; there is nothing else to do. A lot of the locals would go pubbing every night, but you could imagine what sort of condition you'd end up in. I remember doing a bit of it with them but I couldn't see a future in it so it was not for me.

The colours around me are quite stunning, the Chestnut trees with their ivy completely shaded, but somewhere down this path we come out at Stedham and very near Foreshall's old house. Foreshall was head of the first school I went to in Elmsted. The tractor is nervously fussing about, they do fuss these people, I've noticed it before.

The hay wagon at Mother's farm in Chithurst

These Sussex types are terribly twitchy and they drive like hell at night, sometimes at about 80 mph down these isolated country lanes. You hear the bugger coming for ages, watch for the lights and in the wind displacement you realise that if you're unlucky enough to be wondering along the lanes, which I am often late at night, this dude is certainly doing 80 mph so you had better be out of his way as he's totally unaware that other human beings even exist let alone are anywhere near the public highway. I suppose when things are very quiet they rustle along very slowly and then, suddenly there's an explosion, a downpour of rain and suddenly all hell breaks loose or the harvest will be wiped out. Yes, he's busily stacking his bales, which are being made into bundles, big square ones. Up and down he goes, got the trailer nearly fully loaded, then over the hill and towards the pylons which run across Chithurst Farm, mother's old farm just a mile or two from here.

These are the pylons, which go across Hammer Pond to the top of the headland and then down towards Portsmouth. Such enormous power lines. A pity because I think it killed the farm for poor old mother. When she saw them she found it hard to adapt to these modern ways, particularly when it is not your way. We could be on the very edge of Hammer Pond. It's awfully similar, same vegetation, same climate, same place but somehow I'm more pleased to be beside the Rother and I'd rather be here than on the Hudson.

Left the Hudson far behind for a while, sad thing to see that place burn and bake and become so polluted.

Another broken tree, right across the river, just the way it did at Chithurst. It looks exactly the same. We'd get the scouts in at this time of year during their summer vacation who turned these things into bridges. Something for them to do, they'd have their campfires and singing at night, living with nature and learning to survive without TV or electricity, camcorders and video games. What is to become of this generation who are completely ridden with all this technology? Artificial gadgetry. Some work in sometimes, but it does seem to have the capability or potential of destroying the mind. I mean how can an imagination function amidst such awful noise?

We're at Stedham Park now where this beautiful tennis court opposite is part of this estate. It has always been beautiful here as we make our way towards the end of this walk remembering times gone by. It's my time gone by, perhaps Oversby is time gone by. Who is Gerald Oversby? He was my best friend and he was homosexual. Made advances to me and I told mother. Mother broke off the relationship, broke the entire friendship. Today that would be viewed as a scandal but she did her best, I think, to defend me because he was older.

She was worried that somehow he would prey upon me, which he did try to do, but she could not trust in nature. Like so many people, they are such believers in it, but when it comes to manoeuvring they will not let nature have its way. I was fortunately far the stronger of the two, being not tempted nor in any way threatened by his homosexuality. We were, deep down, very very good friends. Was he promiscuous? Yes, but only in weakness. Could that weakness have grown to severe perversion? Who is to say? I walked around Queen's Corner again. What an extraordinary name! That is where his home used to be, with a most extraordinary name, "Titty Hill Farm" and it's still there.

We have reached one of the old bridges that span the Rother. So like Chithurst, but this one in fact is much more spectacular. I think it may even be Stedham. It has some three or four arches to it and it's built like a fortress, but more so. A fortress is only made to stand up to some cannon ball or buckshot, Stedham Bridge is made to withstand a hurricane and it could do so without a shadow of a doubt. The river is quite wide at this point, as wide as at Chithurst. I've just remembered we used to fish here for trout. There were plenty around, they lie under the weeds or sometimes lurk in the sun, but this water is cold, I remember looking at it now, one can scarcely believe it's so cold, but it darn well is.

I miss the home at Chithurst and yet I don't. It's gone; it was never mine. It should have been, it was my home for a while and it was where I called home. There's a little house across from here that even looks like Chithurst through the greenery, with its lace leaded lattice windows, deep, tall arched roof and old chimney, a similar period of time.

Much nicer to look upon these old buildings. Inside they're as dark as hell, you need lamps on in the middle of the day just to read a paper and even in the summer we had log fires blazing but it could be quite cold at night. Everything's open, these people haven't even heard of air conditioning so their doors are open right through. I'm looking through the front

Chithurst Manor was sold to the late Robert Bolt and his wife, Sarah Miles, who still lives there today. Coincidentally Robert Bolt was my English Lit. teacher at Millfield School.

door, which is wide open, and out through the back door, which is also wide open as are all the windows. It's a little smaller than Chithurst but it's been modified and somebody's sitting in the doorway with I fancy a beer bottle. That's one way to kill time. High on the little hilltop here a very unusual sight, beehives 1, 2, 3, 4. Beautifully shaded under and surrounded by chestnut trees. It's just a little hillock but lovely place for them to be and they must like that.

Looking up the Rother River from Chithurst Manor

This dude on the left of the hill has a small chicken coop. He has is own deep litter. Very much natural farming. Amazing how W.R. Grace noticed the potential value of guano whilst working in Peru all those years ago. It made him his fortune.

There are repairs to the edge of this bridge.   Engine drivers, that goes back to the days of steam! 'Notice is hereby given that locomotives are not allowed to stand on any part of this County Bridge', July 1912, West Sussex County Council. 'Any person posting bills on any part of this bridge will be prosecuted'. The good old days. How things have changed! They've rebuilt the western edge of this bridge very neatly, but totally out of keeping with the history. It obviously needed serious repair and it got it.   Just surprised how deep the river is at this point, you can only just get a kayak under this.

So here we have it the River Rother at Stedham, just some two miles away from Bepton and the farthest end of Hamilton's Walk. We don't have to go far to get to Scrimgeour Hall, or whatever my friend, Mallory, calls it and here it is across the fence, my friend's Scrimgeour Hall, no Stedham Hall, of course that's its name, Stedham Hall. How could I forget! It's enormous and looks rather like Worth Priory, where I also went to school.

Stedham Hall

A spectacular sight, Stedham Hall, which tries to be Tudor, with it's huge chimneys, raised roofs, lots of beams and then, underneath at the base, blocks of sandstone. Mallory was absolutely right when she said, "it tries to look Tudor ", but it is nowhere near the right period.

The pylons fade off towards Chithurst. It's not for me. Iping is where I come in and where I go out. A part of me belongs here, but none of me belongs to Chithurst. Yes, I may go back to Hammer Pond just for a quick reconnoitre, but I doubt it. I don't think there's anything left there any more.

Two miles from here is Chithurst and that's where we're going now. In between the narrow walls of Iping Bridge, the narrowest of the lot, one car can just pass with inches on either side. We scrape through and come to yet again to another Church. This one's called 'St Mary's'. This is St Mary's, Iping; the next one will be Chithurst. It's never used and there it stands in all its splendour as we make our way up the hill to Borden Wood, Hammer Pond and Chithurst.

My connection started with Iping. My first encounters and the intimate relations were at Iping but now we go two miles, if that, and we're already on the lane to Chithurst with Hammer Pond on the right. We're heading due west, although I would have said south, but the sun is absolutely in the right position so we're heading due west. The pylons will soon be going overhead.

So much of this road has now fallen to pieces as we look down on the Sussex Downs, with Chichester on the far side and Goodwood slightly to the left. Down into the Dingle Dell, which has always been like a railway tunnel, the trees absolutely touch and join at the top so that even in the afternoon it is dark and down we come to the base of Hammer Pond and Hammer Cottage. Memory Lane, this is it for me.

A quick look takes us down to the tributary, which marks the boundary of mother's farm. This little hill by Hammer Cottage is covered in rabbits. They're like rats crawling everywhere.

Hard to believe we're on the same planet as the Hudson River and the 'Donna Marie', my boat, which is moored there; but suffice it to say we're now suddenly surrounded by mud. I could be very adventurous and take the car over to the right of it but there's a kind of construction down here which is grinding away, some kind of a water pump and yet there is this mud. Where from? What from? Must be to do with this obstacle thing which is pumping water from this tributary up to the hills above Hammer Pond, they rise about fifty feet.

The tributary is looking very bare and there's this old footbridge carved out of a large log across onto Chithurst Farm, whoever it belongs to now. Once mother's, but no longer for I sold all this in '94. It was fun doing it as it was an exercise in business administration I guess. Sold the whole darn thing in two weeks flat. That was my brief, I had nothing else to do at the time so I was glad of it and it was a most successful adventure.

Rather sad to see it all gone now. So the sad memories of Margaret and her entrapment at Windygates (Chithurst Farm), being sort of locked into that bedroom from which she never escaped. She spent I think her last twenty years there. I've been in the US for fifteen so that's a pretty accurate assessment. Occasionally she would get out and go for walks or go to the flat at Child Street, but she never escaped that bedroom. She became committed to it in a lonely isolated way, like a prisoner.

Last turn out of Hammer Wood, the other side of the lane would be Upper, so this is Lower Hammer Wood which comes out onto Hammer Cottage, Maynard Taylor's home for a while, a weekend haunt. It looks pretty different now with modern windows. A humble little building, quite happy to be passing by this one and on up the lane to the top of Chithurst. My old home, but not any more I'm actually glad to say. Time moves on and so shall we. Terribly rough this lane, it's almost like a New York street, but so narrow that one car can just squeeze through here.

There's Bob Collins's smallholding, still in the same place. What does the sign say "duck eggs" and he's called it Hammer Field, about four or five acres with pylons riding over the top of it. This was our headland at the top, some of the best farming land of the whole of Chithurst Farm. The old houses on the left here have fallen into considerable decay.

The Sussex Council used to repair and maintain these roads but since the Thatcher administration all those things have been taken away. You have to repair the bit which you live near yourself now, so it's full of holes and completely fallen through in some places.

Our last twin curves and Chithurst Manor. Horse droppings, as always, in the road and the old church. Seems quite a bit of activity here, three cars are in the driveway. The hedge has lost all its shape. Long way gone, St Mary's Church, Chithurst Farm is remarkably much the same, absolutely overgrown with nettles and weeds; just the way mother would have wanted it! What a mess.

The little bridge, our bit of the Rother. 'Private garden' it says. On through our little town and before you know it we're in Trotton and from Trotton I suppose we'll go to Elsted. Sharp little turn this, a lethal bend, absolutely blind with nowhere to go. Gosh, if you learned to drive here, and I suppose I did, you had no choice but to get it right. If you did this wrong you were dead. I don't remember hearing of people killed but there were some pretty bad accidents, absolutely cannot swerve anywhere. You either sense your head-on traffic and you take immediate and evasive action or you have a fairly good collision, certainly enough to get you into quite serious trouble.

Heading towards Elsted now, Judy Forshall's school. Forshall being the family of which Scrimgeour was the main name, Scrimgeour being the the main occupant of Stedham Hall, which we had been looking at the end of Hamilton's Walk. So we've done quite a large loop all to the west of Midhurst. Now on our home front we find huge cornfields on either side, several feet high, as we come to what is left of this little village. If it ever had a name, I can't determine what it is. Mill Lane, I remember that, unsuitable for motors, but still part of Trotton I guess. Another two miles, at Nyewood we turn left and head for Elsted and Harting on our way back to Bepton, so we're now absolutely square on with the South Downs.

They're quite an impressive sight, not very high, but they have their own unique shape and fauna about them. The Wiltshire Downs are isolated, they are bare but these grow a lot of trees and hedges. This place is absolutely the English version of a jungle, I mean it is crawling with growth. T-junction coming up so now we are forced to make a decision, right to Elsted or left to Ingram's Green. That used to be our old telephone exchange, Ingram's Green 46 was the number at Chithurst. Elsted 1 mile. There used to be a bicycle shop down here, I remember getting my Phillips Sports Populi tuned and readapted here. We're on the home straight, passing Diddling.Funny little place Diddling. You go back to Diddling and I'll go back to doodling, never did know what to do with these weird little names.

So all this introduced me to Goodwood and the start of my racing career. I don't think I ever raced at Goodwood except once in a Formula Junior and, again, in my early days with Porsche. Yet there was this tremendous attraction as a spectator. Funny how a thing can take on a completely different dimension, from audience to participant. It should have taken me a while to learn this circuit even without the disgust of that Moss accident.

There were other drivers who were also tremendously interesting, all of them killed. Hawthorne, Collins, Ivor Bueb, Archie Scott Brown, Stuart Lewis-Evans, on and on. Dark days of racing, it was like a war. The casualty rate just got more and more voluminous as time went by and I began to realise that obviously I had to be one of them. Simple odds.

They were the hairiest days of motor racing, the '60s, the number of serious accidents, Ivor Bueb taking over from Archie Scott Brown in the Lister team. Somehow I took a shine to that, little realising that not long afterwards my engineer, engine builder and maintenance man, Don Moore, was Brian Lister's engine builder/mechanic. He was a very nice, modest, quiet sort of man but not my cup of tea. I need to be around people of considerably more violence, such as Jim Russell who looked like he could have exploded at any minute. Somehow he and I got on terribly well together. He taught me almost everything he knew about driving, racing tactics, shoving people off, getting in the way and not backing off.

The only problem was that he himself never knew when to back down and I also had the same trouble, so I could see that Russell was going to push me into a serious accident, which he himself had had. Damn nearly died at Le Mans, third degree burns driving a 2-litre Cooper Monaco with none other than Bruce McLaren.

Jim Russell (left) and (above) Jim with Steve Lancefield and the CooperMK9

This was real racing. Once it's in your blood and you've got here, to Goodwood, there's no question of backing down. If you get killed, tough; if you get burned, too bad. You just get on with it. It was somehow a sort of a phobia or fever. You were here to bloody race and win.

Russell and I parted company after two years because I could see that he never knew when to back off and, of course, I didn't either. I was too young, stupid and macho, so that's when I went to the 904 and became mixed up with Don Moore, a very mild, sweet character. Our first race was at Brands Hatch, which I drove strictly to orders; but that didn't last long because the next race was the one here, where I took on Lumsden and his very fast lightweight E-type. Moore was rather shattered by all this lot. Not quite geared to the violence of this track. Takes me back to all those names that have passed on. We have other words for it but it certainly was, to put it mildly, a violent activity. High speed and a lot of guts.

The red bike just flashed by, we were looking at it earlier, this beautiful Ducatti, which had been laid down by the slightly aggressive rider we came across earlier who broke his thumb. One can get away with an injured thumb, frankly it beats going to the mortuary. That always used to actually quite surprise me, not the accidents that did occur and I saw more than my share of them, but the ones that you got away with. The chequered flag is out, haven't seen one of those in years. This thing is going too fast, I think it's the Kawasaki. It's very quick indeed.

From here to my second job ever at the Blue Star Garage in Chichester. The owner, Charles Page, was very keen to get racing. Like Don Moore he was another meek, mild mannered man so the closest he got to racing was driving an Austin Healey Sprite and I was salesman. The garage failed. I was one of the first to go so I moved on to Downham.

I survived two years at Jim Russell Racing Drivers School. He said it was time to "pull my finger out". That was always the expression he used. "You know what your trouble is, don't you?" It was always advisable to say "no". He was certainly a rough diamond, but an incredible character. "You want to pull your bloody finger out," he would say. "You've got to get your finger out". I never did say, "What on earth are you talking about?" Anyhow, getting the finger out in this context meant getting into professional motor racing, boots and all, and that's what I did.

On our left, Chichester and, looking at Woodcote Corner, the Porsche 904 and our shunt. Don Moore, Lister's engine builder, just a few years away. I always had a fancy for the Lister Jaguar. I don't why in particular. I liked the colour of the yellow and green livery and the fact that somehow the Lister Jag was an underdog. You had to look at the array of the Astons; there were nearly always three. Moss and Salvadori would be a steady item.

Tony Brooks, Stuart Lewis-Evans and Jack Fairman in this and Jack Fairman in this scene were invincible, so the Lister Jaguar used to come down and take them on. After Don Moore and I almost parted company I had several shunts, which were all unnecessary. They were mostly my fault.

We took the 904 out to Cape Town and there, lo and behold, in the pits all full of smiles and delighted to see me was Charles Page from the Blue Star Garage. "Oh, did I want the car washed?" and he would immediately do that. No, it didn't need washing but I was pleased to see him. He took over and his wife, Valerie Davidson, did the stopwatches and ran the pits and, by gosh, I know that Porsche was a little Teutonic tank but it proceeded to win all its classes and various categories with no bother at all. So that was a very memorable occasion. Its first shunt, here at Goodwood and then probably its moment of glory was the win the next year with Paul Hawkins at the Rheims 12-hour, when we came 6th overall compared to the big cars.

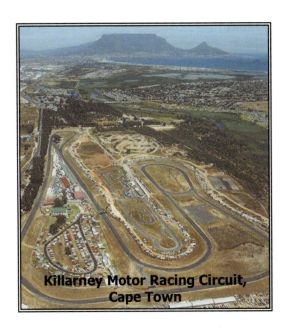

Killarney Motor Racing Circuit, Cape Town

It was a bit of a slow one and it was very heavy but it had endurance, the Carrera 904 G.T.S. It may not have been terribly fast, but you got to 150 in a straight line MPH/2 LT. It was no mean feat.

That win at Rheims was pretty incredible; it was one of Porsche's greatest hours. Hawkins and I were a good match together driving in this 12-hour Rheims 1965. Don Moore actually went on strike. Good old England in the '60s. I had forgotten, but he had taken umbrage at the fact that Hawkins did not acknowledge his pit signals which were given to the driver down at the hairpin pits. The speed had been so fast that you could neither see, nor be seen by signals so any form of communication whatsoever was absolutely impossible. The straight at Rheims was considered as fast as Le Mans because you had to go up a small hill and then you proceeded down quite a steep one. Not the three and a half miles of straight like Le Mans, but this hill took you up to the same speeds. In the case of the Lola T70, 220 miles an hour went through the trap.

All of them Surtees, myself, Hawkins, Epstein and one Sid Taylor, in the 7-litre Ford, which eventually won. We didn't need the signals anyway but, too funny, when they withdrew from the track. They had done a magnificent job of preparation and building the imported engine, so it was a superb win.

Not many wins in ten years I have to say, but some people are lucky and seem to be in the right place at the right time. I can honestly say that winning is all about that. You may have the ability, the courage and the skill but there's still more to it, an enormous amount of luck. Things sort of either shine for you or they don't. You can have an insignificant accident, like Alberto Ascari's Ferrari whilst testing at the Modena track. Went off in a cloud of smoke. Nobody thought anything about it; it was a very small circuit. He did not reappear and so they went around to see where this wreckage was. He was dead, he broke his neck, so this business of winning constantly is a myth in my opinion. There are a few people who have and somehow the forces of nature have conspired to make it possible.

The case in point here at Goodwood, not to depart too much from the theme, is still often considered by many, Stirling Moss. The greatest of all, but he never became a World Champion. He won this and he won that. He was easily the fastest driver, but he was never in the right place at the right time to become a World Champion. He came second in the Vanwall one year to Mike Hawthorn.

After that Hawthorn retired, killed himself on the A3, very near here at Guildford, driving to London in about '59 I think. I was on the Julio Cesari, which we boarded at Cannes en route to New York. I will never forget the stunned shock.

I suppose we had daily newspapers. I can't imagine how the Julio Cesari had daily newspapers, maybe it was by radio, I can't remember, unless they could actually print their own type of paper. I think some cruiser ships did this, but there it was, headlines, the place we had left behind, my old home.

Mike Hawthorn, Britain's first World Champion driver, aged 28 and having retired, was killed on the A3 on the way to a BARC lunch at the Dorchester. Killed on the Guildford bypass near Coombs Garage, Coombs being a frequent entrant of Cooper, usually Monacos, driven by Roy Salvadori. All this connects here, these incredible legends in their time. I mean things like that just didn't happen, ought not to happen, but we were with Moss, never a World Champion.

There were lot of other people who could; Salvadori is a lovely case in point. He definitely had everything that it would have needed to be a World Champion, but I think he didn't want to. He enjoyed his days and won the odd race here and there. Somehow you could tell by the way he conducted himself that he was 'gonna win this one'. No question of backing off, an incredible character. Did more and spent more time at Goodwood I suppose than really anybody else.

There's a lovely little park quite near the top of the pits where I am recapping all these events. Mixed memories, mixed emotions. Memory's not so mixed but the emotions are, the good and the bad, the ups and the downs. There were so many, good and bad. Hard to actually give them a slot, but for me it all began here with Major Barker Bennett. He took me to my first and maybe second and third race meetings. From thereon I got myself here somehow, on one occasion with Philip Borman, my tutor at Windygates, who became fascinated in motor racing. He's still a current friend of mine and is a most interesting fellow who lives in Canberra. I am lucky in that I can say 'here we are at Goodwood'. I have been there, I have done these things. I have seen them win and lose and the winners are the lucky ones. All of us at some point or other have the skills to win. Make no mistake I won a few. No big deal, that's what you go there for, terribly competitive because of the imminent danger.

I think there is no question of anybody backing off, so it becomes a terribly macho/win-at-all-costs sport because this pressure is exerted upon you, but things happen at the end of the day. A guy gets a puncture, a wheel comes off, somebody spins in front of somebody else and takes them off the track with them, or there's a puddle of oil left on the track. All the odds, all the obvious results are thrown out of the window in a second because of these strange events.

Bruce Halford is another of the great Lister Jaguar drivers, after Ivor Bueb. Bruce Halford seems to have taken over, Ivor having been killed driving a Formula 2, of all things, at Monaco. He was an absolute king here in the Lister.   Just extraordinary, sports cars seem to suit some people. Then he drove the 3.4 and 3.8 Jags and the Mark II's like nobody else. He, Salvadori and a mix of others. It was anybody's race really, but certainly Bueb would be right in there with Salvadori, Salvadori probably more often than not coming out the winner. He went on from Aston to Cooper becoming Cooper's Manager.

Brabham started sometime later, so Salvadori did the testing first and then a lot of the driving. He didn't seem so interested in Grand Prix, whereas Brabham was. Jack Brabham's first Championship was in Cooper's first race at Indianapolis, which was then a very small car with a Coventry Climax engine. The big guys then were Vanwall, Ferrari, and Maserati. All front engine stuff, with the driver sitting well and truly behind the engine and gearbox, in between the rear wheels. This was how Salvadori was last seen, in the same sort of get up, with this beautiful thing. I saw it photographed at the end of that season.

It must have been '59 or '60 when the two and half litre limit ended. This year-old untried, or unraced I should say, Aston finally appeared with Salvadori, fully tested and ready to go.

86

It was absolutely a year out of date, it missed the Formula and everything. Really rather a shame, it would have been a very definite contender. So Salvadori you see was somebody who was unlucky in some ways like that. Very loyal to the companies and he always stayed with whichever company it was. Then it was Cooper, then Cooper fielded, Formula 2, then Formula 1. Brabham came along and proceeded to do terribly well, but he didn't seem to cause undue alarm to Salvadori. Always, I would see him here. He would appear in this extraordinary little car, the Cooper Monaco. The world's first rear engine, rear wheel drive, very slippery, ugly looking Sports Car thing, but absolutely invincible compared to the front engines of DBR1-300 and various other Lister Jags, THE sports cars at the time.

This little Monaco, with Salvadori driving it, would just go out on its own and pull away from the field, seconds a lap with ease in the wet or the dry even though it was underpowered, but they never took it a stage further. It was John Coombs, who entered the best of those it seemed to me, certainly looked the best prepared.

I was driving a Formula Junior one time round here, it was pouring with bloody rain and Salvadori went screaming past me shaking his fist. I couldn't see him and inadvertently got in his way, but the speed at which this thing went by was impressive. One could have expected to have been standing still really, the Cooper absolutely flew by.

We were a bunch of little juniors, all slipstreaming together. What a sight, Salvadori in the Coombs Monaco. He could almost be here now.... All these people gone, moved on and all the casualties, the accident in '55 at Le Mans, etc, etc.

I have heard some say he is still around, this legendary Salvadori. Lives in Monaco and lives a pretty gracious sort of a life, probably has a yacht there, who knows, hangs out with some who do. Of all the people that I can name over years gone by that we have seen here at Goodwood, I suppose Salvadori is the most memorable.

One cannot somehow turn a chapter of Goodwood away without thinking of him and yet they all came here, even Edgar Barth, Porsche's best, or so they said, test driver. Colin de Beaufort, Von Trips, I've seen them all here.

Hawthorn, Collins the list goes on and on, anybody who was a driver, even my old J.R, Jim Russell. I say this because of the motor racing school. He coached and taught me really everything I knew. That's actually where I met Frank Gardner, another incredible character with remarkable ability.

Jim Russell had poll position here one day in this Formula Junior race. Funniest thing I have ever seen, even looking at this road now, it's too narrow. I cannot believe how they get away with it. I almost want to try and say how wide it is. It can't be more than 20 feet, it really can't, possibly 25, but not more than that.

The field of a Formula Junior race in those days, that must have been about 1960 or '61 [Lotus 21], was about 30 or 40 cars. I am looking now at the actual grid position. You can get 3 and 2 and 3 and 2 and that's exactly how it was. So we've got 1, 2, 3, 4, 5, 6, 7.......16 rows. Boy, oh boy! Let's call it 15 and factor that by 3, that's the size of the race. I think that this is what had unnerved Jim Russell, anyhow, he had poll position. He wheel-spun off the line, so hung about a bit. Behind him, Peter Arundel, Lotus's works Formula 1 driver at the time, dropped the clutch, jumped the start and shoved Russell so hard up the 'ass' that he spun 180 degrees into the oncoming traffic who then proceeded to peel him, divest him, of every wheel on this little car.

One ran over the top of the car and across his shoulder, missed his face by inches. It was just an absolute pile of scrap. The entire field launched into him and a few others.

I don't think that anyone was hurt, maybe one or two, but just feet away from where I'm now looking was this pile of destroyed Formula Juniors, Russell being one amongst them. About 20 cars without wheels and their engines hanging out. It was the funniest sight I have ever seen. There were something like 5 cars left on this grid out of 35.

Russell got out, totally unscathed, but he did have a bit of a tyre mark over his shoulder. He had a word with the Lotus pit, who all looked very sheepish. He was a physical man Russell, not to be played with. Even if you were the size of John Wayne you still might come off worse if you took Russell on in combat, as they say.

That was to be his last race. He was genuinely quite scared having had a few broken bones and what have you. In his 40s, he decided there and then, right here at Goodwood, to hang his boots up. I went down to him and said he was most welcome to use our garage if he wanted to dump things or leave them there. He was quite nice, he sort of looked me up and down like I was absolute dirt and then realised my intent and well meaning and said: 'No, thanks very much we've got a good transporter, we'll take all this garbage back with us to Snetterton, Downham Market'.

Yet another day, or an anecdote, in the life of Goodwood. I don't think so many cars were crashed in one race at one time. Five cars, then the scraps, the remains, the tyres, the wheel bars, springs and other fibreglass bits were all swept away.

A little known firm had two cars in the lead at this stage out of what was left, maybe five in total, Lolas. Of course I was to become very well acquainted with Lola much later on in the late '60s. So, the Lola was 1 and 2 and it was still pouring with rain at that stage. It usually is because the downs here, from where you see the horse track, face due north. To your left it is due west; it's a classic geographical set up and so, right behind here, if I turn my back, is south; so, ordinarily you know where the wind is, but I didn't in those days I hadn't started flying aeroplanes yet. If you know what the wind is doing - the horsey people know this very, very well indeed - you know exactly what weather is coming your way.

So it's nearly always raining or it's always going to rain here, it's a major factor in your racing at Goodwood. You'd better know your weather and be prepared for it and then you will win. So, all these things are a factor. The fact that you are a good driver or not is almost irrelevant. It'll help, but sometimes it can even be a hindrance for those who know they're good, or think they're too good. They can be pushed into making mistakes. The type, and I've seen plenty, who have the ability and all the attributes are often not good under pressure.

They've tended to climb the ladder rather easily, having more ability than most and were not strappers, like Jim Russell, who, under pressure, is absolutely lethal. The sort of person that you just back off from because he's not going to crack ever under pressure. If he cracked it would be due to a heart attack or something outside his force. So these people with natural ability, Moss was one of them but Moss was always an exception to every rule, would tend to crack under the strain. Some people say that that was the reason Moss never did become a World Champion because, when the cards were really down he would often go off the track, or make mistakes.

I don't think that it's an academic argument, you'd have to spend a few years at a university studying every single statistic available, but it was quite plausible because of Moss's inability to win. In 50% of the races he started in his finishing result was appalling, but he had everything else. So a lot of people, and I use this by way of an example, who have got the ability do not respond well to the pressure of motor racing.

So many memories… and here we have a learner driver's car, with Millers. I passed my test with Millers. Mother made me go to Millers of Chichester. There it goes, a tiny little red car. Not even sure what it is any more, but on it goes onto the track under the main grid and pulls up to a standstill. I think the man at the wheel is the instructor; the young lady is about to have her first driving lesson. This is a fabulous idea. It's what I did with Mrs Smith, you need to be in wide, open spaces as a beginner so that you're not intimidated by hitting things. We all know that the beginner has no car control, otherwise why would they be learning? Yes, this older man is definitely giving her the old one-two instructions. Funny little car, probably Japanese.

In the old days there used to be a pub down here among the paddocks. It was a very small one, as a matter of fact I'm not sure it was a pub. Maybe it was, but it was mostly tea and coffee things. All the people would congregate just down from where I am now, very near McLaren's shrine, and talk about the day. All these people had a magnificent sense of humour, to even engage in such a past time, good or bad, you needed this sense of humour. It's the one bond that held everything together and some of these characters were very, very funny. They had the natural ability to climb aboard a stage and deliver a monologue second to none, put Karl Marx in the shade. Some were raconteurs, some weren't. Moss always was quite amusing, but had his own peculiar way of looking at things so he was always great value and very worthwhile listening to. That would consume some time. Liquor was never really much of an item here, it used to be at other tracks. I remember, it was rumoured that Hawthorn's famous watering hole was 'The Bricklayer's Arms' in Midhurst, which I have been to several times.

Rather a grotty little pub, a typically smelly, dark, very Tudor-styled ancient English pub. All right if you like warm beer, which most do, that's the attraction. He would then go bombing off home at great speed, breathalysers hadn't yet been introduced yet.

I'm waiting patiently for this man to get through his business with Millers Racing School, he's brought out a large notepad, which he now starts to turn over. So many of these people teaching do like to talk ad nauseam, rather than get-on-and-do-it. One of the things that attracted me enormously to motor racing was that really this is a get-on-and-do-it kind of sport. There isn't much time to talk. After the day is over, when your things are on the trailer and your tools are put away then OK you can, but you've got to get home, it's probably sundown, or getting there. Today's expression is very much 'hands-on', it used to be 'get on and bloody well do it'. Hawkins used to say 'when the flag drops, the bullshit stops'.

I don't know where he got that from but it absolutely sums up the situation... nothing to add. Emulate on top of that, 'very much a sport of doers', 'hard price to pay'. I used to feel it with this sport but now, years later, some of the anger has died away. I wasn't as successful as I wanted to be or could have been. This annoyed me immensely. I made a lot of mistakes and I had more than my share of crashes.

I took some appalling bloody risks and I'm lucky to be alive and relatively in one piece, but I had quite a measure of anger in me because of that and I didn't really feel that it was a sport. I thought it was something else. It liked to call itself a profession, because money was starting to be injected into motor racing at a very high rate, whereas now, as I write this book, the famous, like Michael Schumacher before he has even rolled a wheel is the highest paid just standing still. Eight million dollars, it's a sport of big bucks. It can even make the horses and other people look small time. It's outdoors, it's fairly physical. You have to climb on board. It is a sport, but no longer a Grand Prix circuit, maybe never was. Outdoors, changing wheels, tuning and all of that.

Goodwood, I think more than most places I've been to around the world, always thrived on the participation. The crowds could come and look at the pits at certain designated intervals and join in. This wasn't so much the Goodwood 'winning at all costs'; it was about being a sport, taking part and joining in motor racing, timing, giving pit signals and flag marshalling. All the aspects of being involved.

This man from Millers is still going on, I can't believe it. Millers, Chichester Driving School, he's still talking. A little Tiger Moth, beautiful thing, comes flapping in here. Got quite a nice head-on wind so it's working quite hard, behind the barn, there she is, just touches down –

beautiful old thing, probably for a touch and go. If I look slightly to one side we can see whether it goes around. There's another hangar, but I can hear… goodness me, like a helicopter it has gone shooting up into the air again. Already at 100 feet, 200 feet, heading due west in a slight right-hand drift, so she's got the wind head-on. Can't see the windsock but the way the little bi-plane is behaving, it's climbing like a helicopter. What a gorgeous sight. So, all this, somehow now, with the little airport and all the go-karts and the skidpan, this has really made motor sport its home.

Just to be here to see all the funny things you can do now and that old awful thing I was caught up in the 60's, Goodwood, which was why so many people were killed. There were so many accidents. This 'win at all costs' philosophy, which Russell, God bless his heart, tried to instil in me. I thought, you know, to use an Americanism, it's a crock. That's not quite right, it's close, but it's not right. Of course I like winning, but it's not for me, it will never be 'at all costs'. There was too much going on. There's the weather, the scenery, there's the horseracing on the downs, there are so many people involved in just making this thing possible and the flag marshals. I could not possibly 'win at all costs' and that's what is fun about all these various people here. They've got something in common. Motor racing, they like a good time.

This fellow is going round in his Land Rover, all beautifully painted out, unlike the old days. It's got 'Pirelli Goodwood Circuit' on it. Man from Millers is still talking. Absolutely incredible, that is not how you teach people to drive! I didn't spend much time talking to Mrs Pearl Smith I can assure you; I just made her do it by driving round the car park, backwards, forwards and sideways.

A picture is worth a thousand words, an amazing statement. Goodwood. It's about sport, motor sport, it really is and it always was, although the winning was never the prime motive at Goodwood in the old days, or now. Just to get out there, to do it and experience that wonderful form of escape.

The Tiger Moth is coming again for another touch and go. It does seem to flap around quite a bit and yet there's not a cross wind; maybe he's just a beginner. I think he must be, just doing his circuits. Anyway, very steady... over the top of Woodcote, down into the field, you can almost see it touch. He's certainly doing a very nice landing, beautifully under control. Past the hangar, he has indeed touched down.

So all that has made this extraordinary thing, this sport of motor racing and certainly quite a big chunk of my life. It all started here. The early visits, the attraction, the sort of liking to win but hell it ain't everything. Being there, doing these extraordinary things, the machinery, the eccentric people and it certainly does have its share of very eccentric people.

The Lotus Cortina is going away on its trailer. That's how it used to be. We used to watch them all go home on their trailers. The odd, really smooth punter would have his very sophisticated transporter. They had transporters which are more luxurious and better equipped than a coach. Those were the days when the trailer was the modus operandi, even the Listers arrived in trailers. Aston, I think, must have had a transporter, one of the only ones. My God, those things cost several Rolls Royces. Had everything on board, could even make coffee. We've seen the transporter come and go and, of course, the best, BRMs and the Ferrari's, they must have come with their own transporter. Nothing terribly impressive, it was nearly always a Fiat, very Italian. What was always so nice about the Italian entry was that in those days everything was Italian, very nationalistic.

So that is our afternoon at the races. It's an afternoon out, a day in the country. Almost a cloudless evening here. Recounting the extraordinary experience of getting into and out of motor sport, all of which I did here at Goodwood forty years ago and to come back, look upon it, talk about it and wonder at it. The Millers Driving School instructor is still talking, and the one that I did most of my lessons with, Miller, I'm sure is no longer with us.

He was a nice man. I think he was called Arthur Miller, anyway he was very good. A portly man, white hair and a white moustache, but he knew his stuff. Made me drilled and disciplined, which they seem to do in Britain, but they definitely don't in America. You stop at the same place at the same time and look for the same piece of paint. You put that car like it was a rifle through the bull's eye; that was the kind of standard and accuracy. Miller's man is still talking. He's got the pen in the right hand, the pad in his left. You would wonder what on earth he's still droning on about!

Here we have a Chevrolet ambulance no less! Neatly parked inside. So this is all very upmarket compared to our old day. They've got good gear here. They've spent big money on making it very functional. They've done a lot of work and made amazing improvements. The whole thing being a place to get into professional motor racing, not necessarily to have a Grand Prix, just to be a sort of local or home for motor sports, which it is, it absolutely is. Very nicely done and all of first class quality.   They're still constructing more aluminium beams for these various enclosures being built.

Anyway that was our afternoon at Goodwood, in recollection. 10 years of motor racing, always fun. A lovely day out and then somehow the day is gone. It's all over and you're back to square one.

I'm wondering about this peculiar wooden construction here, this is how they now enter and exit. Doesn't have a paddock as it did at the far end, I should say the south end. This is some kind of platform. There is a starter's flag; maybe it's where prizes are awarded. They had something like this at the Nürburgring so many years ago.

My visits to the Ring were not pleasant. One was with the 904 and Hawkins, we were a very strong pair indeed and quite capable of taking anyone on. This was the only time my mother rang me abroad anywhere, to announce that my father had died. She even found the Gasthof Penta!

This was a big international race and all the guys had lined up in the Zodiac wagon waiting for me to go and surprise, surprise Mrs de'Udy was on the line. Extraordinary things that people do, to announce that my father had just died. Some people would find that very hard to deal with, but I am not emotional...in the normal sense. Motor racing always came first. It's fun, but its dangerous and the stakes are always high. They're higher than you think; it just has to come first. There is no question about it and if you are surrounded by people who don't understand us, they have to be gotten rid of immediately. They literally don't belong; they're not going to make it. They not only don't belong, but they can't participate.

You all have to know that and that is one of the major problems between all these people. Motor racing comes first and here we are not necessarily talking about the winning thing; but if you're going to do it you must realise the high stakes, the dangers, the breakages and the things that can go wrong before you've even started, but motor racing must come first. That somehow is what gets you together.

This peculiar psychosis, if you like, is what overcomes class, race prejudice and religion. Any of those sink into the background with this title and theme, which literally lays down the law. It is a law; it's like a physical law. Motor racing comes first. Whatever you do, if you're a flag marshal or a timekeeper, people have to unite, particularly feminists. Minority problems where these angry women, black people, gays and lesbians who demand their fair share which they haven't had. They're usually right, possibly so, but life still doesn't owe you a thing.

Then, at the other end of that scale, here we are doing this funny activity. I had to be good to penetrate all those sorts of ideas and that is the theme of today vs. motor racing, it comes first. It's in the right place. It has always been, never been anywhere else but here.

We're at Goodwood at the end of the day and nearly everybody has gone home, but the gates are still open. Not like the old days, these are open. You could come round here and lap round the circuit. I don't know what they'd do now; somebody would eventually stop you I suppose because there are people cutting grass and clearing up and all that. I wonder if our Miller's Driving School man is still there talking. The odds are he is, but it's rather sweet here now this private enterprise owned by the Earl of March. He is still there, Millers Driving School, still talking! This poor lady's chances are next to zero if you have that for a driving instructor.

Uncle Sam's has managed to climb in on the act as well, not stupid those people. Then, way down near the end of course, the famous old emblem. Something rather special about it, Aston Martin. Aston Martin did race here. Based at Feltham, which is south of Heathrow, this was the nearest track for them for testing, developing and testing all kinds of gear. Even for all of its shortcomings, this was their home. No wonder their sign belongs over there in its premier position, Aston Martin. This is it, Goodwood. It was their place, their testing ground. If any Aston was to succeed it would have to succeed here; it would have to work here. Again, the old do-and-die thing.

Now I can see the Cathedral spire very clearly, almost due South, but it is slightly to the West, and you can't see the rest of the City. Like Midhurst it has sunk into a valley, and yet there is no valley at Chichester. There is a valley at Midhurst and Midhurst is well and truly sunk into that. No wonder at my first cross country flight, where we set out from Blackbushe, I got to the triangle so I picked Midhurst as opposed to going from Midhurst. I was to proceed to Winchester for the second point of the triangle and then back to London. I mean it is almost impossible to describe what the world looks like from an aeroplane as we are at this very moment. All this, very, very tight to the land, as much as fox hunting and all those other sports.

So obviously I never found Midhurst, but I did find Chithurst, my old home a couple of miles away, but I was by then a few miles off course. Well I suppose I did find Winchester, or something like it; that was the second point of the triangle. The third point, I arrived back in the London area right in the middle of Heathrow's control zone without knowing where the hell I was and out of fuel, flying a thing called the Beagle Pup which was fully aerobatic. I knew that under me was the main Reading road; it had to be the A4, which was the main road to Bath and Bristol in those days. If things were really tight, this is the point to do the 'do-and-die' thing.

Not as much time to talk about this problem, as our Miller's Driving School man, I would have to do an about-turn, 180 degrees, and land with the traffic, which I think would be no major accomplishment at all. It was quite easy, but you have to make this decision in seconds and be prepared to execute it.

Anyhow I sent out an emergency call and they were awfully nice. Heathrow: 'Are you lost?' Me: 'yes'. Heathrow: 'OK, turn 90 degrees west', which I did; '90 degrees East', which I did. 'We have you on radar, you may now proceed' and they gave me a bearing to Blackbushe from my supposed position. That was something, again, I shall never, ever forget, my first cross-country flight just a few miles from here.

So then, things link up. Bermuda, Iping House, Chithurst, our day at the races, our day at Goodwood, motor sport. It begins and it ends here. Goodwood motor circuit, somehow so special it's rather hard to describe. It has improved tremendously since our day in the'60s, but motor racing was very serious indeed. Still, it was a sport and the people came here to have a good time. It was very competitive but it wasn't, even then, the 'win-at-all-costs' scenario which you would find at Brands Hatch, Silverstone and Monza. Obviously Ferrari must win at Monza, the Italians go absolutely berserk if Ferrari doesn't win at Monza. It's practically a lynch mob! You absolutely have to win.

It's nearly time to withdraw. Our little adventure, almost a séance for me, is over. Our reach from here, to Kyalami, our near win with Gardner and I in the Lola. All such a thing of the past now. Sometimes I wonder if it wasn't over ages ago, or if one imagined it all. We did climb the ladder, we certainly did, Gardner and I were definitely there. How to win and, if not, to win consistently I think that was always the winner. If we were to arrive at the track you'd presume we'd be the ones to beat.

That was a unique feeling and that didn't come overnight. Oh, there was a lot of work involved. I must say I have no regrets on this, the equinox, of 1999. My moves were made with the best of intentions, whether they succeeded or failed is not even relevant.

Thank you for reading my story and I hope you enjoyed remembering the old days/ways of motor racing in the 60s/70s.

I have written another book called 'My Side of the Story' in which I talk more about my racing experiences, mishaps, co-drivers and other amusing incidents during my racing career and which includes most of the photos and newspaper articles from my collection.

Michael de'Udy

Me in the Porsche 904 passing Jackie Epstein in his Ferrari LM275 at the 3-hour race on Boxing Day, Pietermaritzberg 1965. My brakes cooked on this occasion so I couldn't carry on. Pietermaritzberg is where Mahatma Gandhi was born and in the film you see him being physically thrown off a train there for sitting in the 'Whites Only' compartment!

I know the routine,
can't you drop another quarter in the machine
I'm feelin' so bad,
can't you make the music easy and sad
I could tell you a lot
but it's not in a gentleman's code
So, make it one for my baby and one for the road.

Extract from:
"*One for My Baby and One for the Road*"
Sung by Frank Sinatra,
written by Harold Arlen and Johnny Mercer

Michael Grace De'Udy, United Kingdom

General figures
Years of activity: 1964-1970
Number of races: 82 (including 2 races where did not start)
Total entries: 82 (contains 46 finishes and 32 retirements, finishing ratio: 58%)

Achievements
Wins: 9 / Additional Class wins: 15
Second place finishes: 10 / Third place finishes: 4
Races finished on podium: 23
Best result (count): 1st (9x)
Pole positions 5

Notes of interest
Most frequent co-drivers: Frank Gardner (14), Peter de Klerk (8), Hugh Dibley (3), Paul Hawkins (2), David Piper (2), Peter Westbury (1), Mike Hailwood (1), Colin Davis (1), Jimmy Blumer (1)

Most frequent makes: Porsche (39), Lola (36), Ford (6), Ferrari (1)

Most frequent types: T70 (36), 906 (27), 904 GTS (12), Mustang Boss (6), 250 GTO (1)

Most frequent chassis: SL73/105 (17), 906-129 (15), 906-101 (12), 904-085 (11), SL73/112 (10), SL76/149 (8), SL76/138 (1), 3757LM [250GTO] (1)

Most frequent tracks: Kyalami (8), Killarney (7), Roy Hesketh (6), Silverstone (6), Crystal Palace (5), Brands Hatch (5), Lourenço Marques (5), Kumalo (4), Zeltweg (3), Vila Real (3), Nürburgring (3), Mugello (3), Castle Combe (2), Sebring (3)

Most frequent countries: ZA (24), GB (24), I (6), MOC (5), D (5), RSR (4), A (3), P (3), F (3), USA (2), B (2), NL (1)

St. Louis, Missouri: Bruce Tuffly invited me to see his restoration work on my old 906.

Beside my Porsche, now owned by Terry Hefty as one of his collections

" It's the result that matters."

Reims 1965

Sunday 11⁰⁵ am

1ˢᵗ G.T. Class under 2000 c.c.

2ⁿᵈ G.T. cars overall.

6ᵗʰ Overall 12 hour marathon.

Me and Paul Hawkins. Big Class win in overall 12-hours Marathon with Porsche 904 in Reims 1965

Porsche 906 making its debut in 1966 at Castle Combe near Bath. One of a hundred Porsches they made. John Aldrington changing the front wheel.
Photo courtesy of Alan Giddins

Africa: de Udy/Gardner again-

Mike de Udy speeds his Lola T70 Mk 3B to its second successive Springbok win which, with his co-driver Frank Gardner, has now secured him a firm lead in the series after only three races.

Lourenco Marques 3 Hours:

De Udy/Gardner again

Mike de Udy/Frank Gardner (Lola T70) pull further ahead—John Love retires—Walker/Widdows (Ferrari P4) second

By DAVE CLAPHAM

Drivers having won with Lola T70 M3 GT

Frank Gardner won 8, 5 with me

Top left to right:
Frank Gardner (Aus) 8 wins;
Denny Hulme (NZ) 6 wins;
Paul Hawkins(AUS) 6 wins;
Brian Redman(GB) 5 wins

2nd left to right:
Michael de'Udy (GB) 5 wins;
Chris Craft (GB) 4 wins;
Joachim Bonnier (S) 3wins;
Teddy Pilette (B) 3 wins

3rd left to right:
John Love (ZA) 2 wins;
Richard Attwood (GB) 2 wins;
Jean-Michel Giorgi (F) 2 wins;
David Piper (GB) 1 win

4th left to right:
Mark Donohue (US) 1 win;
Chuck Parsons (US) 1 win;
Jackie Epstein (GB) 1 win;
Trevor Taylor (GB) 1 win

Bottom left to right:
Ronnie Peterson (SW) 1 win;
Ulf Norrinder (SW) 1 win;
Jean Pierre Beltoise (FRA) 1 win;
Wilson Fittipaldi (BRA) 1 win

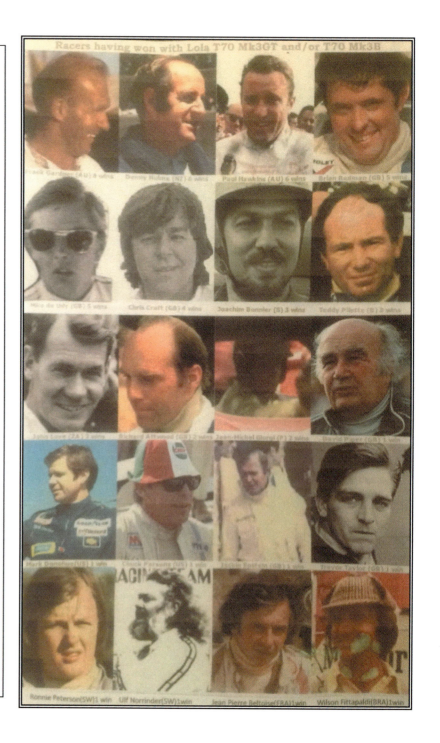

**Me at Brands Hatch BOAC 500
LAST RACE!**

**Me co-driving with Frank Gardner.
Together we won the Lorenzo Marques 3-hour race in Mozambique**

GERHART MITTER: King of the 906
Gerhart taught me how to drive the Nurburgring.

Lightning Source UK Ltd.
Milton Keynes UK
UKIC01n0056030714
234466UK00006B/47